ATTORNEY WELLNESS ADVOCATE

*Elevating Legal Professionalism
with Holistic Health Practices*

Kimberly Busch

Inspire Legal Publishing

Inspire Legal Publishing

CONTENTS

We have never arrived. We are in a constant state of becoming.

—Bob Dylan

Become An Attorney Wellness Advocate

Imagine embarking on a journey toward a new mindset that could radically alter your understanding of success. As a lawyer and professional, you've invested countless hours in your craft, honed your skills, and reached notable heights in your career. But what if you're just beginning to explore what's truly possible? What if, despite your accomplishments, there's an untapped reservoir of potential waiting to be discovered?

This isn't just another wellness book. This is an invitation to a transformative experience that aims to redefine your perspectives, rejuvenate your body, and enhance your mental faculties, all while elevating legal professionalism through holistic health practices.

For many, the pursuit of success often comes at a cost. Long hours, intense pressure, and endless commitments can lead to a neglect of health and well-being. It's a common narrative: the successful professional who has everything but whose physical body bears the brunt of relentless stress and neglect. You might consider yourself at or striving towards the peak of your career, yet feelings of being stuck or stagnation may emerge. This should be taken as a signal. Your body and mind are craving more than just professional achievements, and they're highlighting the necessity for a deeper engagement with your well-being. This scenario invites you to view wellness not merely as a supplementary aspect of your daily living but as a core foundation of your success and life.

It's a common misconception that physical health operates in a vacuum, separate from professional success and mental acuity. Recognizing the intricate relationship between these elements is crucial to accessing unprecedented levels of performance and fulfillment. We delve into how physical well-being significantly bolsters mental and emotional health, cultivates clearer thinking, and boosts professional efficiency. The interconnectedness of our physical state with our cognitive and emotional well-being underscores the profound impact of each health-conscious decision we make.

Moreover, it's essential to clarify that excellence in one's profession is not exclusively the domain of those in perfect health. Individuals navigating health challenges, disabilities, or chronic conditions embody remarkable resilience and determination. This book is crafted for anyone on the spectrum of health and wellness, advocating that improvement and personal bests are achievable regardless of the starting point or physical limitations. This message is one of inclusivity and empowerment, affirming that striving for better health is a journey accessible to all, and each step forward enriches not just our personal well-being but also our professional lives and mental agility.

In the realm of wellness, certain topics often remain in the shadows, yet they hold profound significance for our overall health. Fascia and the lymphatic system are two such elements of our anatomy that, despite their vital roles, are frequently overlooked. Fascia is a continuous web of connective tissue that wraps around our muscles, bones, and organs, providing structure and support while facilitating movement.

This dynamic, living tissue is not just a passive framework; it plays an active role in our flexibility, immune response, and overall well-being. Fascia's intricate connection with the lymphatic system, a crucial network responsible for detoxifying the body and maintaining immune function, underscores its importance. Together, these systems form the foundation of our physical health and have a profound impact on our mental and emotional states. By understanding and nurturing these systems, we can achieve a harmonious balance that enhances every aspect of our lives, from preventing pain and injury to fostering emotional resilience and overall vitality.

Many of us, even the most well-educated, experienced professionals, tend to delude ourselves and our thinking when it comes to health and wellness. We know what we need to do, but it is very easy to prioritize work and family to make excuses to neglect your own physical and mental health.

Prepare to challenge your preconceptions, explore new dimensions of determination, and discover strategies that will not only change how you work but how you live and advocate for your own wellness. Whether you're reaching the peak of your career or looking to overcome a sense of stagnation, becoming an Attorney Wellness Advocate will guide you to a more integrated, vibrant, and extraordinary professional and personal life.

Does It Make Sense To Separate Mind And Body?

In the realm of wellness and personal growth, particularly when considering a professional practice, the distinction between the mind and body often blurs into a seamless continuum. What we traditionally perceive as the mind, encompassing our thoughts, emotions, and consciousness, is indeed an intricate symphony of neural activities within the brain, an undeniable part of our physical being.

Modern science and ancient wisdom alike advocate for a more holistic understanding, one where the mind and body are not separate entities but rather facets of an integrated whole. This perspective is crucial for professionals who navigate a landscape where mental acuity and physical stamina are intertwined. The stress experienced during a high-stakes courtroom trial, for instance, isn't just a mental or emotional state; it manifests physically through a quickened pulse and tense muscles. Similarly, the physical act of a mindful yoga session can lead to mental clarity and reduced anxiety.

If you are experiencing feelings of depression or a sense of stagnation, engaging in physical activities can be an effective step toward improvement. While physical exercise is not a panacea, it is well-documented that enhancing your physical condition can have a positive impact on your mental and emotional well-being. It's important to clarify, however, that while improving physical health is beneficial, it should complement, not replace, any prescribed treatments or medications. Always consult with healthcare professionals before making changes to your treatment plan. They can provide guidance on how best to integrate physical health improvements with existing medical treatments to enhance your overall mental acuity and state of mind.

By adopting practices that nurture both mind and body, legal professionals can enhance their cognitive function and physical resilience. This enables them to manage the demands of their careers more effectively and sustain high levels of performance. When lawyers are healthier and mentally stronger, their improved interactions have a ripple effect throughout the profession. This enhances not only how they treat clients and colleagues but also elevates the collective reputation and standard of the legal community as a whole. Thus, fostering holistic health is not merely about individual improvement but about uplifting the entire legal profession through enhanced professionalism and mutual respect.

This comprehensive approach to wellness ensures that caring for the body and calming the mind are not isolated acts but part of a unified strategy to foster well-being, enhance your capacity as a legal professional, and enrich your life in every dimension. This nuanced understanding of health and well-being reveals the interconnected nature of the mind and body, suggesting they are beautifully and complexly intertwined, perhaps even one and the same.

In the legal profession, where ethical conduct and self-regulation are paramount, the ancient yogic concept of the Eight Limbs of Yoga offers a profound parallel to the holistic development of a lawyer.

The first limb, Yamas, resonates closely with the ethical guidelines that govern attorneys. Just as the Yamas provide ethical precepts such as Ahimsa (non-violence and compassion), Satya (truthfulness), and Asteya (non-stealing, akin to respecting client trust accounts), they mirror the foundational ethical obligations of lawyers to act with integrity, honesty, and respect for others' rights. Incorporating these values into daily practice fosters a law practice rooted in fairness and ethical responsibility.

Moving to the Niyamas, which emphasize personal observances like Saucha (purity) and Tapas (self-discipline and zest for life), lawyers can find guidance in maintaining mental clarity and personal integrity, crucial for handling the complexities of legal work. Santocha (contentment) teaches lawyers to find satisfaction in their work regardless of external rewards or recognition, fostering a sense of fulfillment that is internally driven.

The third limb, Asanas, or physical postures, traditionally associated with yoga, serve as a reminder that physical health and mental acuity are interconnected. For lawyers, maintaining physical fitness can enhance stamina and reduce the stress inherent in high-stakes legal environments. Engaging in regular physical activity, whether through yoga or other forms of exercise, supports not only physical health but also mental sharpness and emotional resilience.

The remaining five limbs of yoga: Pranayama, Pratyahara, Dharana, Dhyana, and Samadhi, each contribute to the cultivation of a more focused, serene, and insightful legal practice. Pranayama, or breathwork, is essential for managing stress and maintaining emotional balance, offering lawyers techniques to remain calm and centered even in the midst of a trial, complex deal, or negotiation. Pratyahara involves the withdrawal from sensory distractions, a valuable skill for attorneys who must often ignore extraneous information to focus deeply on the task at hand.

Dharana, the practice of concentration, directly supports the intense focus required for legal analysis and long hours of preparation. Dhyana, or meditation, helps deepen this focus into a profound state of contemplative insight, fostering a clarity of mind that can greatly enhance strategic thinking and decision-making. Finally, Samadhi, the state of complete enlightenment, represents the ultimate integration of one's personal and professional growth, where heightened awareness and deep peace pervade all aspects of life.

These advanced practices of yoga are not merely exercises but are profound tools that can significantly improve mental resilience, analytical depth, and personal satisfaction in the legal field. Each limb will be revisited in specific contexts throughout the book, illustrating how they can be practically and beneficially integrated into the daily lives and professional routines of legal practitioners.

This holistic approach, integrating the Eight Limbs of Yoga with legal practice, encourages lawyers to see themselves not just as practitioners of law but as whole beings whose professional lives are deeply connected to their personal growth and well-being. By fostering a balanced lifestyle that honors ethical integrity, personal discipline, and physical health, legal professionals can enhance their capability to navigate the demands of their careers with greater clarity and effectiveness.

Ancient Wisdom For A Modern World

In the midst of our current era, where technological advancements have reshaped virtually every facet of our lives, we find ourselves at a crossroads. It is indeed an extraordinary time to be alive; the conveniences afforded to us by modern technology are unparalleled. With just a few taps on our smartphones, we can access the collective knowledge of humanity, summon goods and services from across the globe to our doorstep, and connect with people thousands of miles away instantly. This level of accessibility and convenience is unprecedented in human history.

However, this remarkable era of instant gratification and

digital omnipresence comes with its own set of trade-offs. In our rush to embrace the future, we've inadvertently distanced ourselves from the ancient wisdom that has guided countless generations before us. The practices, rituals, and insights that have served humanity for millennia have been overshadowed by the allure of a world where everything is immediate. As a result, we find ourselves grappling with the unintended consequences of our modern lifestyle: diminished attention spans, reduced capacity for deep focus, and an increase in physical ailments such as eye strain, muscle stiffness, and the chronic neck and back pain associated with endless hours in front of screens.

This disconnection from ancient wisdom and the natural world is not without remedy. The principles of health and well-being that our ancestors understood intuitively, grounded in harmony with the natural world and a deep connection to one's own body and mind, remain as relevant today as they ever were. It's becoming increasingly clear that in order to navigate the challenges of our digital age, we must rekindle our relationship with these timeless truths.

Reflecting these challenges is the stark reality that, in the United States, life expectancy has begun to decline for the first time in a century (National Academies of Sciences, Engineering, and Medicine, 2021). This alarming trend, marked by increases in mortality from conditions like heart disease and metabolic disorders, often exacerbated by the obesity epidemic, underscores a crucial disconnect.

As we advance technologically, we must not lose sight of the fundamental health principles that sustain long-term well-being. The rise in mortality rates, particularly among working-age adults, signals a pressing need to address the lifestyle choices and environmental factors contributing to this decline. Our pursuit of modern conveniences should not come at the expense of our health; instead, we must strive to integrate ancient wisdom with modern practices to create a balanced approach that enhances our overall quality of life.

Chapter 1: The Cumulative Impact Of Daily Habits

Understanding stress and its profound impact on our physical and mental health is not just a matter of personal well-being; it's a crucial factor in professional competence and longevity. The legal profession, known for its intense pressure, long hours, and complex cognitive demands, places attorneys in a unique position regarding occupational stress and its consequences.

The implications of elevated stress levels in attorneys are multifaceted and far-reaching. High psychological demands have been significantly associated with personal and work-related burnout. Furthermore, attorneys are particularly susceptible to secondary traumatic stress due to their extensive exposure to clients' traumatic experiences, which can lead to symptoms akin to PTSD, such as anxiety, emotional overwhelm, and difficulty concentrating (Love, 2017).

Given the evident high levels of chronic stress, burnout, and secondary traumatic stress among attorneys, addressing these issues is not merely an individual concern but a professional imperative. Initiating self-care practices before symptoms become debilitating is crucial. Attorneys and firms must consider strategies to mitigate these stressors, including workload management, seeking and providing adequate support, and promoting a culture that acknowledges and addresses the mental health challenges inherent in the legal profession.

It's imperative to highlight the role of daily habits in constructing our physical and emotional well-being. Each decision, from adopting moments of mindfulness to managing workload, acts as a foundational building block. Like a structure relying on the integrity of each element, our capacity to handle professional pressures is shaped by the cumulative effect of these daily practices. The ensuing sections will explore how these habitual choices, often perceived as minor or routine, are pivotal in sculpting our resilience and effectiveness, both in our careers and personal lives, emphasizing the transformative power of small, consistent actions.

Small Bricks Shaping Your Physical Person

Almost every trial lawyer I've ever met describes their legal strategy for a case as building a wall brick by brick. Just as every small piece of evidence is a necessary brick in the wall that is the case, our daily habits are the small bricks which combine to form the structure that is our physical body day by day. As legal professionals, we understand the importance of each small element that might seem unimportant individually, but cumulatively will compound into a formidable wall of evidence. Similarly, you can use this same mindset to examine the daily habits that constitute the structure of your physical body, mind, and life.

Each day presents a series of minute decisions: what to eat, what to drink, when to work, how to unwind, how to move your body, what time to go to sleep. Individually, these choices might seem insignificant, as you likely will not notice the difference of a single choice, or even a series of choices over short periods of time. The fact that each small decision alone makes a (seemingly) unmeasurable difference in the big picture can lead to excuses and self-deception.

We fool ourselves by saying it doesn't matter if we do this one small thing this one time that does not serve our greater goals. Just as each brick is critical to the integrity of a structure, these daily choices accumulate, building the person we become. It's in these small, seemingly insignificant everyday decisions where we carve out the person we want to be. Every brick counts, and every brick built or stripped away will be moving the structure of your physical body and mind towards a positive or negative trajectory.

Through this lens, it's evident that the construction of a strong, resilient structure, whether a legal case or our well-being, requires attention to detail and a deep commitment to consistency. Each correct or poor choice is like choosing high-quality bricks or flawed ones that might crumble under pressure. By recognizing the significance of these daily choices, we can build a healthier, more robust self that stands firm in the face of life's challenges, much like a well-constructed wall stands the test of time.

Instant Gratification Vs. Long-Term Satisfaction

Understanding the differences between the benefits and consequences of instant gratification and long-term satisfaction is crucial when you are willing to take an honest examination of your daily habits. These choices, often made in the pursuit of immediate comfort or pleasure, underscore a broader psychological narrative about how we navigate decisions in our lives.

Instant gratification is compelling; it promises immediate rewards with minimal effort. Common examples where this might manifest are the quick hit of energy from a sugary snack or the immediate sense of relaxation from a drink after a stressful day. While these choices can offer temporary relief or pleasure, they're akin to short-term fixes that don't address underlying needs or consequences. Over time, the cumulative effect of these decisions can lead to negative outcomes such as poor health, decreased mental clarity, and even professional burnout. The momentary pleasure they provide is overshadowed by the long-term toll they take on your well-being.

Over-indulging in short term gratification is a sign of immaturity; it is common among children, teenagers and young adults. It can take time, mistakes, and life experience to develop the wisdom to appreciate how the long term-consequences outweigh the temporary and fleeting nature of instant gratification. Some of us adults, however, may need a reminder (I include myself in this group).

Good habits may not deliver the same immediate buzz as instant gratification, and they may require some short-term sacrifice, but they are the path to lasting satisfaction and well-being. Choosing a balanced meal over fast food, engaging in outdoor exercise over doom scrolling your phone, or prioritizing quality sleep over a night out might not provide instant gratification (although they can!), but better choices offer profound benefits over time. These habits contribute to a stronger, healthier body, a sharper mind, and an overall sense of well-being. They require more effort and discipline initially, but the long-term rewards are immeasurably greater.

To transition from prioritizing short-term pleasures to embracing long-term well-being, a shift in perspective is needed. It involves recognizing the deceptive nature of instant gratification and the enduring value of good habits. Understanding that each choice you make is an investment in your future self can motivate you to opt for healthier options, even when they require more effort or discipline.

Further, once you have gotten more attuned to your physical body by taking better notice of your habits, you may find the positive daily habits do, in fact, offer a form of instant gratification in a more satisfying way. For example, once you have reduced your intake of ultra-processed food, you may realize how energized you feel almost immediately after a healthy, whole food meal. Once your body is conditioned to a higher level of cardiovascular fitness and strength, you may experience an endorphin rush, also known as the runner's high, during or after your workout (no matter what form of exercise you choose.) And who doesn't feel great upon waking up after a satisfying night's sleep?

Mindfulness is a powerful tool in this transition. By becoming more aware of your choices and their impacts, you can start to break the cycle of instant gratification. Practices like Pratyahara, Dharana, and Dhyana are particularly effective in cultivating this awareness, and they are discussed more fully later in this book. Pratyahara teaches you to withdraw from external distractions, allowing for a deeper focus on the present moment. Dharana, the practice of concentration, directly supports the intense focus required for legal analysis and long hours of preparation. Dhyana, or meditation, refines this concentration further, fostering a heightened state of consciousness and enabling reflective thinking.

Pause and consider the long-term effects of your decisions.

Ask yourself whether a momentary pleasure is worth the potential long-term consequences. Use logic and stop making excuses or outright lying to yourself. This mindful approach to decision-making can help you build a foundation of habits that support your health, well-being, and professional success.

Consider this a journey of construction and growth. Reflect on the habits that constitute the bricks of your days. Are they laid with care and intention, leading you toward the person you aspire to be? Are they supporting your health, your mind, your career? If not, it's never too late to start laying each brick with purpose, to begin building (or rebuilding) a foundation for the future you desire. This is your life, your case to present, and with each deliberate, daily decision, you have the power to create continuing growth and improvement to be the best version of yourself you can be.

The Misplaced Priorities Paradigm

In the realm of high-pressure professions, the prioritization of work often overshadows a crucial component of life: personal health and wellness. Moreover, many professionals would state their family as their top priority in life. That's fair, but it's important to care for yourself so you can care for others, the same reason airlines advise you to secure your own oxygen mask before helping others. We need to shift this paradigm to urge professionals to confront the reality of their lifestyle choices and to approach their health with the same rigor and dedication they apply to their careers and familial obligations.

Now, you may be thinking, "But my family *IS* the most important thing to me, and I have to *WORK* to support them, and

I therefore don't have time for exercise, eating healthy, or getting enough sleep." If you are using these obligations *as excuses to neglect your own physical and mental health*, you will not truly be putting your family or career first. What if you prioritize your own health and well being. Wouldn't your family life and career be bolstered as an additional positive consequence of improved daily habits and actions? This book argues that it would.

Long hours, intense focus on client needs, and the perpetual chase for professional success often lead to health being sidelined. Moreover, this way of thinking can even be elevated to bragging rights: how many billable hours we've logged, how little sleep we've had, how early we arrive and how late we leave. Partners and associates at a law firm typically do not brag about the great 8 hours of sleep they got the night before when they are in the midst of trial preparation (or any day, really).

The pursuit of career success and financial stability, even with the noblest of intentions, can lead to a dangerous trade-off: short-term gains at the expense of long-term health. Working excessively long hours and neglecting physical and mental well-being might yield immediate professional accomplishments, but this often comes with a steep price: a decline in health. There are countless stories of individuals who, upon reaching the pinnacle of their careers or at the dawn of retirement, find themselves unable to enjoy the fruits of their labor due to health issues that could have been mitigated or avoided altogether.

Professionals, especially those in law, are trained to face hard truths, critically examine evidence, and provide realistic advice. However, when it comes to our own personal health, there's often a disconnect. Many of us are in denial about the state of our health and the long-term consequences of our lifestyle choices.

It's time for a reality check: to assess health with the same critical eye used in legal analysis.

Think about your own habits and their eventual consequences as if they are facts in your legal case that do not support your side. You don't ignore those facts, hoping they just magically disappear. You know they will be brought up against you eventually. So what do you do? You confront them head on, you bring them up first, and you figure out how to deal with them. Just as one wouldn't ignore crucial evidence that is not in your favor, it's imperative to not turn your back on the negative evidence in your own case of physical health and wellness. Face it, deal with it, change it.

Health Investment For Career Excellence

Viewing health as the ultimate investment in your career is crucial. This investment is not merely about extending one's lifespan; it's about enhancing the quality of life, both professionally and personally. We can all think of examples of extraordinarily successful and wealthy individuals whose lives were cut short by illness or disease. No amount of money can prevent these outcomes.

While illness and death can strike anyone at any time, even those with exemplary habits and in peak physical condition, ignoring risk factors and not attempting to mitigate them is not an option. Good health is not only a personal asset but also part of your professional brand; it enables you to perform at your highest level in your career, to be present for your family, and to enjoy the rewards of your diligence.

Treating your health as you would a complex legal case

can be transformative. Start by investigating your current health status, understanding your lifestyle and daily habits, and identifying areas for improvement. This phase is akin to gathering evidence. Then, move into the research phase, seeking information on nutrition, exercise, and stress management, much like you would research legal precedents and case law.

The planning phase involves creating a structured, realistic strategy to improve your health. This plan should be as detailed and well-thought-out as a legal strategy, tailored to your specific needs and circumstances. Just as you would meticulously prepare for a case, approach your health plan with the same level of detail and precision. This might include setting specific goals, scheduling regular check-ups, planning balanced meals, and establishing a consistent exercise and sleep routine.

Consultation with experts, such as doctors, healthcare professionals, personal trainers and fitness coaches, is akin to seeking specialized expert advice. These experts can provide insights and guidance tailored to your unique health profile. You wouldn't build the case without consultation with your expert witnesses, right? Use this book as motivation, but then turn to medical, nutrition and fitness experts in your own life to help you navigate the complexities of your unique situation, ensuring that your plan is not only effective and fits into your schedule but also sustainable in the long term.

Building on the understanding that personal health should never play second fiddle to professional obligations, it's crucial to address a common narrative within the legal community. This narrative, deeply ingrained yet increasingly challenged by recent events, suggests that the demanding nature of legal work leaves little room for health and wellness practices. An article from the ABA Journal in 2015, prior to the seismic shifts brought about by the COVID-19 pandemic, sheds light on this very dilemma. It underlined a pervasive belief among lawyers that despite knowing the importance of sleep, diet, and exercise, the relentless pursuit of billable hours and professional success often leads to the neglect of these fundamental health pillars (Gordon, 2015).

Yet, the global pandemic has acted as a catalyst for change, emphasizing the importance of health and introducing greater flexibility into the professional landscape. This newfound flexibility, encompassing remote work, home offices, streaming video meetings, and more adaptive work schedules now offer legal professionals unique opportunities to integrate those healthful practices long deemed unattainable.

The journey towards a healthier lifestyle is not about making excuses but about embracing the opportunities for change that recent times have presented. The pandemic has taught us the value of adaptability and the critical role of health in professional excellence. This period of global upheaval has not only highlighted the feasibility of maintaining healthful practices amid a busy legal career but has also underscored the importance of such practices in enhancing our overall quality of life and professional performance.

The call to action is clear: lawyers must leverage the lessons learned during this unprecedented time to foster a professional environment where health and success are not mutually exclusive but mutually reinforcing.

This shift in mindset, supported by structural changes within the profession, paves the way for a future where legal professionals no longer have to choose between their career and their well-being. As we move forward, embracing health as an integral part of professional life becomes not just a personal choice but a collective imperative for the legal community.

Chapter 2: Exercise As Training For Life

For many professionals, exercise is often relegated to just another task on an extensive to-do list. Yet, envisioning physical activity not as a mundane item but as critical training for life's demands shifts its significance. This perspective repositions exercise from a discretionary activity to a fundamental practice, preparing us for life's challenges with the same rigor we apply to our career endeavors.

In this context, exercise becomes an essential element of training aimed at bolstering both physical and mental resilience. The legal profession, marked by its demanding nature, necessitates recognizing physical activity as integral to our well-being. This approach transforms exercise from a burdensome task into a potent strategy for empowerment and professional effectiveness.

It's crucial to note that achieving a holistic state of health involves focusing on three pillars of fitness: cardiovascular endurance, strength, and flexibility. Improving your cardiovascular health and muscle development is vital, as poor fitness in these areas is a leading cause of heart disease (the foremost killer of men and women alike, according to the CDC.) If you find yourself gasping for breath during mild physical activities, it's a critical signal from your body to prioritize cardiovascular training and muscle building. Embrace this challenge with the urgency and dedication you would apply to a high-stakes project at work.

Remember, the essence of transforming your approach to exercise isn't about chasing the elusive ideal of athletic perfection or peak physical condition. It's about undertaking a journey of honest self-assessment and dedicating yourself to incremental improvements in your health and fitness. This commitment is rooted in the pursuit of gradual, yet significant, progress rather than an unattainable ideal. It's about the accumulation of small victories, the day-to-day choices that foster a sustainable and balanced lifestyle.

Setting habit-based goals is pivotal in this journey. Instead of vague aspirations, focus on concrete, measurable actions such as committing to a certain number of workouts per week, improving your time or distance in cardiovascular activities, or progressively increasing the weight in your strength training routines. These habit-oriented goals are not only achievable but also allow you to track progress and celebrate the milestones along your path to better health.

Aligning these goals with your routine ensures that exercise becomes an integrated part of your life, rather than a sporadic effort. Let these goals guide your daily actions. By doing so, you create a framework of habits that supports not just your physical well-being but also your mental and emotional balance. Moreover, incorporating physical activities into your daily routine doesn't have to come at the expense of family time. Working out, whether at home, at a gym or outside, is a great activity to do with a partner or spouse. Young children love to be pushed in a jogging stroller and/or ride bikes with their parents, and many gyms offer childcare. If your kids are a little older, inviting them to work out with you can be an excellent way to bond and instill in them the value of health and fitness. Children learn by watching their parents; teach them good habits by practicing them yourself and inviting them to join you. If you are struggling to find time, you will have to adjust your schedule, say no to less important things, and find creative solutions to prioritize cardiovascular exercise and strength training as non-negotiable activities in your life.

For those who might not consider themselves inherently athletic, the process of engaging in regular physical activity can be especially transformative. Discovering one's potential through consistent exercise often reveals a previously unrecognized capacity for resilience and strength. I know many legal professionals who participate in events like fun runs, couch to 5Ks, marathons, or even triathlons aren't elite athletes; they're ordinary individuals seeking tangible goals. Many of us are middle aged or older when we get the running or triathlon bug (I say us, as I myself only became a runner at 36 and ran my first marathon at 41, first sprint triathlon at 43). The act of training for these events, setting athletic goals and striving towards a specific target, not only enhances physical stamina but also fortifies the mind.

This journey of physical exertion and accomplishment teaches valuable lessons in perseverance and self-discipline, qualities that transfer into other life domains. Participants frequently report a surge in confidence upon reaching or surpassing their fitness goals, as they may be achievements they once thought beyond their capabilities. This newfound confidence can catalyze positive changes in other areas of life, leading to enhanced overall well-being. The challenge itself, more than the physical activity, enriches mental clarity and emotional resilience, making the training process rewarding.

Exercise as training for life has the power to change how individuals approach challenges in all areas. The discipline, focus, and persistence developed through a consistent exercise routine can significantly enhance personal and professional experiences. For those who might have underestimated their physical abilities, the newfound confidence gained from surpassing their perceived limits can spill over into other realms, enriching their approach to work, relationships, and self-development.

The Importance Of Muscle As We Age

If we age without sufficient exercise, our bodies will likely undergo a decline in muscle mass, a condition known as sarcopenia, which can have profound implications for our overall health and quality of life. This is particularly significant for professionals who spend most of their day seated at desks, often leading to inactivity that accelerates muscle loss. Understanding and countering this natural progression is crucial for maintaining not just physical health but also for ensuring continued efficacy in demanding roles.

The loss of muscle mass affects more than appearance; it directly impacts stability, mobility, and increases the risk of falls and injuries, all of which can lead to decreased independence and a reduced ability to perform everyday activities effectively. For those in sedentary professions, maintaining muscle strength through a balanced exercise regimen that includes cardiovascular fitness, strength training, and flexibility exercises is integral to both personal well-being and professional performance.

Engaging in regular cardiovascular exercise helps improve heart health and increases stamina, while strength training is crucial for preserving muscle mass and bone density, enhancing metabolic health, and boosting energy levels. Flexibility training, such as yoga or stretching routines, complements these activities by improving joint mobility and reducing the risk of injuries, ensuring a well-rounded approach to maintaining physical function.

Setting specific, measurable goals for each aspect of your fitness is important: cardiovascular endurance, muscle strength, and flexibility. These goals could range from increasing the duration of a cardio session, improving the amount of weight lifted during strength training, or extending the reach in flexibility exercises. Tailoring these goals to individual needs allows for gradual and sustainable progression in physical fitness.

Incorporating a comprehensive exercise regimen is a powerful way to combat the natural effects of aging and maintain high levels of physical and cognitive function. This commitment not only counters muscle loss but also serves as a proactive measure to enhance overall life quality. By prioritizing muscle maintenance and setting clear fitness goals, professionals can ensure they remain sharp and ready to tackle the challenges of their careers with vigor and resilience.

Muscle maintenance is a professional necessity, not just a personal health matter. Viewing strength training, cardiovascular fitness, and flexibility exercises as essential components of a health-focused lifestyle allows professionals to maintain their physical abilities and cognitive sharpness. This holistic approach to fitness empowers individuals to perform at their best, enhancing both their personal lives and professional capabilities.

Embracing Cardiovascular Fitness

Cardiovascular exercise is a cornerstone of any well-rounded fitness regimen, essential not only for fitness but for basic health. The heart is a muscle, arguably the most crucial one, and like any muscle, it needs to be exercised to stay strong. Heart disease remains a leading cause of death for both men and women globally, making cardiovascular health a priority for everyone, regardless of age or fitness level.

Engaging in regular cardiovascular exercise does more than improve heart health; it enhances overall stamina and aids in the efficient functioning of the respiratory system. Activities such as running, cycling, swimming, or even brisk walking can significantly boost heart rate, promoting better blood circulation and lung function. This type of exercise is especially beneficial as it also contributes to fat loss and helps regulate blood pressure and cholesterol levels.

I know what you are saying: I hate to run! That makes sense. That is exactly what I also said and thought before I changed my habits. If you have low cardiovascular fitness, this type of exercise to increase your heart rate will be difficult and uncomfortable at first.

Fortunately, I can assure you that if you stick with it, and your fitness levels improve, it will get easier. And you don't have to be a runner, in fact, that may be contraindicated for some people with hip or knee complications (if this is you, speak to a health professional or experienced personal trainer to find the right cardio exercise to meet you where you are.)

Any form of cardiovascular exercise will work as long as

you get your heart rate up. If you're engaging in cardio but not breaking a sweat, you may need to increase your effort. Adequate cardiovascular exercise should challenge your breathing; a good tip to know whether you are exerting sufficiently is you should be able to speak but perhaps not sing.

As stated, the initial phase of starting a cardio routine will take a lot of effort. Many people experience shortness of breath, excessive sweating, and even mild nausea as their bodies adjust to the new demands being placed on their cardiovascular and respiratory systems. It's crucial to push through this initial discomfort (while easing up or stopping if symptoms are severe). As your endurance improves, these symptoms decrease, and you might even experience the famed "runner's high," a rush of endorphins that can make the physical effort profoundly rewarding.

Feeling the benefits of cardiovascular fitness in everyday activities can be incredibly satisfying. The ability to ascend stairs effortlessly or enjoy a long hike without undue fatigue enhances the quality of both personal and professional life. Cardiovascular activities such as running, walking, or biking offer more than just physical benefits; they can also be meditative practices that help clear the mind and reduce stress. These activities can be enjoyed alone for introspection or with family and friends, providing a wonderful way to combine social interaction with physical health.

Taking these cardiovascular activities outdoors adds an additional layer of benefit. Exercising in natural environments boosts mood and self-esteem even more than indoor exercise. Whenever possible, I encourage you to step outside and embrace the added sensory experience of fresh air and changing scenery, which can transform a routine workout into a more robust therapeutic activity. You can also integrate outdoor activities into your workday by taking walks during breaks, stepping outside for phone calls, or even holding walking meetings with colleagues.

These small changes not only enhance your physical health but also provide mental clarity and a refreshing change of pace during the day. To fully enjoy these opportunities, investing in appropriate gear for different climates ensures that outdoor activities remain enjoyable and feasible year-round, so weather never becomes a barrier to your cardiovascular health.

It's important to consult with a healthcare provider and/or experienced personal trainer before starting any new exercise program, especially if you have existing health issues. A doctor can advise on safe heart rate targets and any precautions you should take based on your medical history. Tailoring your cardio routine to your specific health conditions and physical capabilities is crucial to avoid overexertion and injuries. For some, lower-impact activities like swimming or stationary cycling might be more appropriate than running, depending on joint health and overall fitness.

Persistence is key in cardiovascular training. The benefits of overcoming the initial hurdle are immense, not just physically but also mentally. Regular cardio can reduce stress, improve sleep, boost mood, and enhance cognitive function, making it a powerful tool for those in demanding professions. By committing to regular cardiovascular exercise, you set the stage for a healthier, more energetic life, capable of tackling not just physical challenges but professional and personal ones as well.

Strength Training Is For Everyone

Strength training, in the past overshadowed by cardiovascular exercise in popular fitness culture, is an essential component of a comprehensive health and fitness regimen for everyone, not just athletes or bodybuilders. Recently, strength training and heavy weight training has been embraced by people of all ages, genders, and abilities. It's a message for all professionals who may not have physically demanding jobs but will benefit from the myriad of positive changes that strength training offers.

The importance of strength training transcends gender and age. Women are increasingly recognizing its value, especially with the growing awareness of the importance of training for muscle and bone health of post-menopausal women. Men typically do not need to be convinced of the benefits of weight lifting but may need help in the execution of the idea. Regardless of gender, incorporating strength training into one's routine enhances overall physical resilience, making daily activities easier and reducing the risk of injury as we age.

For beginners eager to start strength training, it's advisable to begin with fundamental exercises that target major muscle groups. This approach ensures that you develop a solid strength base while minimizing the risk of injury.

Starting with basic bodyweight exercises, done without additional weight, is a practical way to familiarize yourself with the movements and improve your overall fitness as a beginner. If you need to improve physical fitness but otherwise are in good health, see if you can perform these basic exercises and use additional resources easily found online for more help. If these bodyweight exercises are out of reach for you now, I highly encourage you to reach out to a professional to offer specialized modifications and supervision.

Squats are excellent for the lower body, engaging the quadriceps, hamstrings, glutes, and calves. Focus on keeping your feet shoulder-width apart, back straight, and lowering your body as if sitting back into a chair, ensuring your knees don't push past your toes.

Push-ups help strengthen the upper body, including the chest, shoulders, and triceps. If standard push-ups are too challenging at first, modifications such as performing them on your knees or against a wall can help build your strength gradually.

Lunges are vital for developing leg strength and improving balance. They work the thighs and hips and involve the core for stability. When lunging, step forward and lower your hips until both knees are bent at a 90-degree angle, keeping the front knee aligned over the ankle.

Planks are a powerful exercise for the core, crucial for overall stability and strength. They also engage the shoulders and back, supporting proper posture and reducing the risk of back pain.

Once comfortable with bodyweight routines, you can transition to incorporating weights with exercises. Initially using a light kettlebell or dumbbell can introduce you to the form required for more complex weightlifting movements.

By focusing on these exercises, you can build a strong foundation of muscle strength and endurance, crucial for progressing safely into more challenging routines. As you become more confident in your abilities, gradually introducing weights can help deepen muscle engagement and promote further gains in strength and fitness.

Particularly for beginners but applicable to all, the guidance of a personal trainer can be invaluable to learn these basic strength training exercises and many more. A trainer ensures that you are performing exercises with the correct technique and form, which is crucial for preventing injuries and maximizing the effectiveness of your workouts. They can also help in building a personalized training program that aligns with your specific goals and needs. For those who feel intimidated by gym environments or unsure about how to use various equipment, a few sessions with a personal trainer can boost confidence and provide a solid foundation for an independent workout routine.

Furthermore, starting with two to three training sessions per week can help integrate strength training into your lifestyle without overwhelming your schedule or causing injury. Each session should include a variety of exercises that promote muscle growth and endurance, gradually increasing the intensity as your body adapts. It is essential for people who have not done strength training ever, or years ago, to start slowly. You do not want to injure yourself, as that will derail the progression. You can always add more weight and specific training exercises as you continue in your routine over time.

Strength training is essential for everyone, particularly for professionals in mostly sedentary roles. It's a critical investment in long-term health and functionality, ensuring that as you advance in your career, your body remains resilient and vigorous.

For those dealing with injuries or chronic conditions, collaborating with physical therapists or relevant experts can tailor a program that accommodates specific needs, enhancing safety and effectiveness.

This inclusive approach ensures that strength training is accessible and beneficial for all, regardless of physical challenges. Committing to a program that aligns with your abilities and goals not only aids in building a stronger physique but lays the groundwork for a more dynamic and healthy lifestyle. Engaging in strength training is a powerful step toward ensuring that your professional achievements are matched by your physical well-being.

Yoga, But Make It Convenient

When considering ways to improve physical and holistic health, it is essential to strike a balance between cardiovascular fitness, strength, and flexibility, particularly for those in sedentary professions. Yoga, through its asanas, or physical postures, plays a crucial role in enhancing flexibility, which is an integral part of this balance. Traditionally, asanas were developed to prepare the body for meditation, making them a foundational element of the Eight Limbs of Yoga.

While this book primarily focuses on asanas, it is important to recognize that these physical postures offer more than just increased flexibility; they also provide significant mental benefits. Originally a practice developed by and for men, yoga has evolved over time to become inclusive, offering its benefits to anyone willing to engage with its disciplines. This evolution is particularly important in the Western context, where yoga's popularity among women often overshadows its universal applicability. Regardless of gender, the principles of yoga and its asanas remain relevant and accessible to all, providing a pathway to improved well-being.

For anyone experiencing stress as an almost-constant companion, yoga offers a sanctuary. It's vital to recognize that we often store stress and trauma in our physical bodies, manifesting as stiffness and rigidity. Yoga, with its focus on flexibility, can play a pivotal role in releasing these physical manifestations of stress, leading to a decrease in overall tension and an improvement in mental clarity. To put it very plainly, yoga makes you feel good. Acknowledging the misconceptions that yoga requires extensive time commitments or is inconvenient for busy schedules, yoga can be an accessible and indispensable practice...convenient, even.

The end of this book contains sequences specifically curated to integrate seamlessly into the bustling lives of legal professionals, ensuring flexibility can be cultivated by all, regardless of existing physical capability. This approach underlines the importance of flexibility as a universal asset, with many, particularly those more accustomed to rigidity, standing to gain significant benefits.

The benefits of yoga, in its capacity to foster both physical and mental resilience, have been demonstrated in various studies, including one funded by the National Institutes of Health over a three-year period. This research specifically highlighted the significant impact of trauma-informed yoga in reducing PTSD symptoms among women with treatment-resistant complex PTSD (Van der Kolk, 2014). Such findings underscore yoga's therapeutic potential, not just for enhancing concentration and reducing stress but also as a vital tool for navigating mental health challenges.

In response to the challenge of integrating yoga into a

demanding professional schedule, this book encourages readers not only to try the recommended sequences but also to consider attending a yoga studio for a more immersive experience. This dual approach allows professionals to adapt yoga into their daily routine in a manner that best suits their individual needs and preferences. While the sequences in this book are crafted for convenience and accessibility, the immersive experience of a studio practice can deeply enrich one's journey into yoga, offering a fuller understanding and appreciation of its benefits.

This initiative is about making yoga approachable and achievable for those who may have previously viewed it as incompatible with their professional lives. It is an invitation to explore how even the busiest individuals can incorporate yoga into their routine, experiencing its transformative effects on both health and career. By presenting yoga as a flexible practice that can be tailored to fit the constraints of a legal professional's schedule, we aim to inspire a commitment to personal well-being that complements and enhances professional excellence.

Not Flexible Enough For Yoga? Good!

As a certified yoga instructor, the notion that one must be flexible to practice yoga is the most common misconception and response I encounter on the topic. Many people express concerns about their flexibility, or rather, their perceived lack thereof, as a barrier to starting yoga. They often say, "I'm not flexible enough to do yoga." To this, my response is annoyingly enthusiastic: "Great! Being a beginner is an excellent place to be; let me tell you why."

If you consider yourself inflexible, you stand to gain the

most from beginning a yoga practice. Yoga is not about demonstrating flexibility from the outset; it's about gradual improvement and long-term gains. In fact, those who start their yoga journey with limited flexibility often experience the most significant gains in a relatively short period of practice. This rapid progress is not only gratifying but can also be more pronounced than the improvements seen by individuals who have been practicing yoga for years and are already quite flexible.

The beauty of yoga lies in its accessibility and adaptability. It welcomes everyone, regardless of their starting point in terms of flexibility or physical fitness. The practice itself is designed to gently increase flexibility, strength, and balance over time through consistent practice. Moreover, the benefits of yoga extend beyond mere physical flexibility; they include enhanced mental clarity, stress reduction, and an overall sense of well-being.

Therefore, if you find yourself thinking, "I can't do yoga because I'm not flexible," remember that this is precisely why yoga is a perfect choice. Starting your yoga journey from a place of lesser flexibility means you'll be able to witness tangible progress quickly. Each practice will bring you a step closer to a more flexible, stronger, and balanced version of yourself, both physically and mentally. Embrace your starting point with openness and curiosity, and allow yourself to be amazed at how much progress you can make. Yoga is a journey of self-discovery and personal growth, and your level of flexibility at the beginning is merely your starting line, not a limitation.

For those new to yoga, these sequences at the end of this book are an excellent starting point. They offer an accessible introduction to the practice without the need for special equipment or extensive training. However, even seasoned yoga practitioners may find value in these sequences, especially the office-friendly routines that can be easily integrated into a busy workday.

While the sequences in this book are a good introduction to basic yoga postures, they are barely scratching the surface of what yoga has to offer. Exploring yoga further can deepen your practice and enhance its benefits. Local yoga studios are a fantastic resource, offering a variety of classes and styles. For beginners, it's important to choose a studio and class that feels welcoming and comfortable. There are many different styles of yoga, and many personalities of yoga instructors, that appeal to different levels and goals. Don't hesitate to contact studios beforehand to discuss your experience level and what you're looking for in a yoga practice. Most studios are more than willing to guide beginners to classes that suit their needs. If a studio doesn't feel right, remember, there are plenty more to choose from.

Online resources also provide a wealth of information and guidance. YouTube channels dedicated to yoga offer a range of tutorials and classes for all levels, allowing you to practice in the comfort of your own home or office. These online platforms can be particularly useful for busy professionals who may not have the time to attend studio classes regularly.

The perception of yoga as an esoteric practice is not uncommon among professionals. Yet, the transformation many experience upon embracing yoga is both profound and surprisingly practical. Imagine the sensation of a deep, satisfying stretch, akin to an internal massage, unraveling the knots and tensions hidden within your body's fabric. It's an awakening, a revelation for many who never realized the extent of their physical constriction until they felt the expansive freedom that comes with newfound flexibility.

Yoga, in its essence, is an invitation to explore the uncharted territories of your physical and mental landscape, revealing the potential for suppleness not just in muscles and joints but in every aspect of life. This journey towards flexibility and the accompanying sense of liberation is accessible to individuals across all fitness spectrums. The sequences offered in this book are merely a beginning, a gateway into a world where the disciplined harmony of body and mind elevates your daily existence.

Far from being an extraneous addition to your routine, yoga offers a fundamental enhancement to the way you live and work. It's not merely about adopting a series of postures; it's about engaging in a practice that massages your inner self, eases the mind, and prepares you to face the rigors of your profession with renewed energy and perspective. Given yoga's established benefits for individuals of all abilities, the question arises: Why wouldn't professionals, even the most skeptical among us, embrace it with curiosity in pursuit of a more balanced and fulfilling career and life?

Building Consistent Fitness Habits For Active Lives

Before you roll your eyes and wonder if I've lost my mind suggesting you start cardio, weights, and yoga all in one go, hear me out. I promise I'm not asking you to ditch your day job to become a fitness guru overnight. Think of these ideas as nudges towards self-improvement, whether you're squeezing in one new routine or gradually adding more. Maybe life's hectic right now, or perhaps you've got a bit of downtime after finishing a big case or project. Whatever your schedule, these are inspirations for doing a little bit better, not doing it all at once.

In the realm of personal fitness, setting habitual goals is pivotal. Rather than anchoring these goals to outcomes such as weight loss or muscle gain, it's more advantageous to establish them based on the frequency and type of exercise. This strategy encourages a focus on attainable, progressive improvements in fitness rather than fleeting physical transformations. As fitness levels evolve, these goals can be adjusted, promoting a continuous journey of personal development. This approach shifts the emphasis from sporadic effort to consistent engagement in cardiovascular, strength, and flexibility training activities, underscoring the importance of regularity and perseverance in building a healthier lifestyle.

To track and sustain motivation effectively, employing a physical calendar tracking system can be particularly useful for professionals accustomed to meticulous planning and detail-oriented work, such as attorneys. Marking each workout session completed mirrors the practice of noting critical deadlines and appointments, applying the same organizational skills to personal health endeavors.

This method involves setting specific, manageable goals that are easily tracked. For instance, committing to two cardio sessions and two strength training sessions per week, and incorporating a few 10-20 minute yoga practices in between. Whether you find yourself pressed for time during a hectic work week or enjoying a more flexible routine, these strategies are designed to inspire gradual improvements without the pressure to do it all at once.

Placing this calendar in a prominent spot acts as a continuous reminder of both commitments and achievements. Each mark made, whether a sticker or a simple check mark, represents a deliberate action toward better health, akin to ticking off a completed task or meeting on a work schedule. This visual accumulation of daily efforts builds a tangible record of discipline and perseverance, fostering a routine that enhances physical and mental stamina required for demanding professional roles.

The visual satisfaction of seeing a calendar fill up with accomplishments can significantly boost motivation. It breaks down the formidable task of achieving fitness goals into daily manageable activities. Including a variety of exercise intensities, from high-energy workouts to gentler, restorative sessions like yoga or walking, ensures the routine remains balanced and engaging, preventing burnout. This method is particularly powerful because physical changes from exercise, such as increased muscle tone or cardiovascular fitness, do not appear overnight.

The calendar serves as a tangible measure of progress long before physical results are visible. As you commit to and accomplish daily fitness goals, the marked calendar becomes a symbol of dedication and progress, offering immediate visual gratification that compensates for the slower pace of physical changes. Body recomposition is a gradual process that begins at the cellular level, often taking weeks or even months before significant visual results are observed. However, with consistent effort, noticeable improvements in general well-being and energy levels can typically be felt within just 30 days, with more substantial physical changes following after about 90 days. The filled calendar stands as a testament to the effort made, encouraging patience and persistence as the body slowly transforms.

This method does more than track physical activity; it reinforces the disciplined habits integral to legal practice. Each marked day is a reminder of progress made and a motivational push towards ongoing commitment. Just as meticulous planning and foresight serve a lawyer in managing complex cases, they are equally effective in managing one's health. By translating these professional skills into the fitness domain, lawyers can enhance their well-being, ensuring they are as sharp and resilient in their personal health as they are in their legal careers.

Chapter 3: Releasing Stress Through Fascial Health And Breath

The human body is a marvel of interconnected systems, with fascia as a crucial, yet often ignored, component. Our fascia wraps around our muscles, bones, and organs, forming a continuous web of connective tissue. Our fascia network is responsible for holding and shaping our physical body, but it is active tissue that is intricately linked to our lymphatic and immune systems. This network is a living, dynamic structure essential for our flexibility, immune response, and overall well-being, deserving as much attention as any other vital organ.

Fascia permeates every corner of our body, ensuring strength, structure, and the ability to move with ease. However, the demands of high-stress professions, especially within the legal field, can lead to a sedentary lifestyle that neglects the needs of this vital tissue. When we fail to move sufficiently, our fascia stiffens and tightens, leading to discomfort and reduced mobility, impacting our daily functions and overall health.

The fascial system is intrinsically linked to the lymphatic system, which has been described as a "secret river" that maintains health by transporting toxins, immune cells, and biological messages throughout the body (Lemole, 2021). This system relies on good flow to function effectively, facilitated by the muscular movements that also support fascial health. Just as the fascial network supports physical structure and flexibility, the lymphatic system works to nourish and cleanse the body, highlighting the critical synergy between these systems.

Fascia can store stress and emotional trauma, acting as a physical repository for our psychological burdens. This storage capacity explains why practices like yoga and acupuncture can profoundly affect our emotional well-being and stress levels. By releasing tension in the fascia, these practices facilitate the release of stored emotions and trauma, offering a path to healing that transcends the physical, touching the very essence of our emotional health and resilience.

In essence, considering and caring for your fascia is an integral part of a comprehensive approach to wellness. It is a commitment to enhancing your quality of life, ensuring that your body's support and immune system is maintained and nurtured. By prioritizing fascial health, you equip yourself with another strategy to manage the rigors of your profession and promote harmony between body and mind. Embracing this aspect of self-care is a step towards achieving optimal health, enabling you to thrive in all areas of life.

Fascia And The Retention Of Accumulated Stress

In the legal profession, where the weight of critical decisions and intense negotiations is a constant presence, stress is an inevitable part of the job. Lawyers and legal staff frequently face adversarial situations where people's lives and livelihoods hang in the balance. The high-stress environment doesn't just strain the mind; it manifests physically, particularly in the fascial system. Understanding the relationship between stress, wellness, and fascia can be transformative for legal professionals, offering a pathway to improved health and more effective, compassionate practice.

The relentless pressure faced by attorneys and legal staff, from managing client expectations to meeting tight deadlines, triggers the body's stress response. This response, beneficial in short bursts, can become harmful when prolonged. Chronic stress leads to continuous muscle tension, affecting the fascia by causing it to tighten and stiffen. This fascial stiffness restricts movement, creates pain, and further exacerbates stress, creating a vicious cycle. For legal professionals, whose job demands mental sharpness and emotional resilience, this can manifest as decreased productivity, increased error rates, and a generally lower quality of life.

Do you have chronic neck and back pain? Tight and unhealthy fascia is linked to common stress-related ailments manifesting physically that many in the legal field face. Issues such as chronic back pain, neck stiffness, and headaches are prevalent due to long hours of sitting. Furthermore, unhealthy fascia can lead to reduced range of motion and flexibility, making one more susceptible to injuries, which in turn can lead to further stress and anxiety. Addressing fascial health can significantly alleviate these conditions, improving both physical and mental well-being.

For legal professionals looking to break the cycle of stress and its physical manifestations, prioritizing fascial health is key. Regular movement breaks are essential, even during the busiest days. Incorporating short, frequent periods throughout the day to stretch and move can help release fascial tightness and alleviate muscle tension. Engaging in gentle, mindful exercises like yoga not only stretches and strengthens the fascia but also promotes mental relaxation and stress relief, providing a double benefit for those in high-pressure legal roles.

Professional therapies such as myofascial release, massage, or acupuncture can be incredibly beneficial, targeting specific areas of tightness and discomfort. These therapies can release fascial restrictions, improve blood flow, and enhance overall mobility and well-being. If you have never tried acupuncture for stress relief or chronic pain, it can be an unexpectedly eye-opening experience and is discussed in more detail below. Additionally, hydration plays a crucial role in maintaining healthy fascia. Drinking ample water throughout the day ensures the fascial network remains lubricated and functional.

You hold the cumulative effects of years of stress, trauma and emotional clogs in your fascia. When you are able to release some of this tension, you will feel it both physically and emotionally. Releasing years of built up tension in the fascia through stretching, exercise, hydration and proper nutrition should then set you up to heal and grow. By embracing strategies to care for their fascial health, legal professionals can mitigate the impact of stress on their bodies, leading to a more balanced, focused, and effective practice.

Breathwork For Fascial Wellness And Mobility

Navigating the intricate landscape of fascial health, breathwork emerges as a potent and accessible tool for professionals to manage stress, improve mobility, and foster overall well-being. One tool to learn breathwork is yoga, with its integration of breath and movement. This aspect of yoga aligns with Pranayama, one of the Eight Limbs of Yoga, laying the groundwork for understanding how controlled breathing can significantly influence our physical and mental state.

The essence of breathwork lies in its diverse array of

techniques, specifically designed to optimize emotional and physical states of being through deliberate breathing patterns. These practices, ranging from immediate stress-relieving exercises to more elaborate breathing sequences, share a common goal: to manipulate our breathing in ways that positively affect our body and mind, with a special focus on enhancing the elasticity and resilience of our fascia.

Transitioning from yoga's breath-centered postures to the focused discipline of breathwork presents an opportunity to directly target and alleviate the physical manifestations of stress, notably held within our fascial system. Stress, particularly prevalent in high-stakes professions, often tightens and stiffens our fascia, leading to discomfort and reduced mobility. Through breathwork, we can consciously relax and soften the fascia, promoting better movement, reducing pain, and improving our overall physical well-being.

The role of breathwork in maintaining and improving fascial health is twofold. Firstly, it aids in regulating the autonomic nervous system, shifting from a state of stress (sympathetic activation) to one of relaxation (parasympathetic activation), allowing the fascia to release and regain its natural flexibility. Secondly, focused breathing enhances blood flow and oxygenation to fascial tissues, supporting their ability to heal and maintain their structural integrity.

As we explore basic breathwork techniques for beginners, the emphasis remains on their benefits for fascial health. Each method offers a pathway to not only manage stress and its physical repercussions but also to unlock greater mobility, resilience, and a deeper sense of bodily harmony.

This exploration of breathwork within the context of fascial health is not just an addition to your wellness toolkit; it's an invitation to experience firsthand how the simple act of breathing can profoundly transform your physical state. By integrating these breathing practices into your daily routine, you're taking a proactive step toward sustaining your fascial health, ensuring that your body remains supple, responsive, and ready to meet the demands of your professional life.

Stress, particularly chronic stress, initiates a cascade of physiological responses designed for short-term survival in threatening situations, commonly known as the "fight or flight" response. This primal mechanism, while life-saving in the face of immediate danger, can become a source of continuous wear on the body and mind when perpetually activated, as often seen in legal professionals. The stress response floods the body with cortisol and adrenaline, hormones that, over time, can lead to a range of health issues from hypertension to anxiety, and significantly impair the health and functionality of the fascial system, leading to stiffness, pain, and decreased mobility.

Breathwork emerges as a potent tool in mitigating these stress-induced ramifications, offering a bridge to enhanced fascial health and overall well-being. By intentionally manipulating breathing patterns, breathwork practices can exert a profound influence on the autonomic nervous system, shifting it from the sympathetic "fight or flight" mode to the parasympathetic "rest and digest" state. This transition not only diminishes the immediate sensations of stress but also contributes to a long-term bolstering of resilience against stress-related ailments.

Scientific evidence significantly highlights the efficacy of breathwork in mitigating stress, with particular emphasis on Alternate Nostril Breathing (ANB). Studies have shown that just five minutes of Alternate Nostril Breathing (ANB) can substantially enhance parasympathetic tone, indicating a direct influence on the body's rest and digest response (Sinha et al., 2013). Such an increase in parasympathetic activity not only lowers cortisol levels but also uplifts mood, alleviating symptoms associated with anxiety and depression. Furthermore, the relaxation fostered by consistent breathwork practice extends its benefits to the fascial system, easing tension, promoting enhanced flexibility and mobility, and facilitating a sense of physical and mental liberation. For those of us facing continuous pressures as part of daily lives, the integration of ANB and other breathwork practices into daily routines emerges as a strategic method for preserving health and bolstering stress management capabilities.

This direct intervention at the physiological level of stress responses through breathwork, particularly practices like ANB, not only strengthens mental health but also supports the health and vitality of the fascial system. By nurturing a more relaxed and less rigid fascial network, breathwork practices significantly contribute to improved posture, pain reduction, and an elevated overall quality of life. These attributes render breathwork, especially Alternate Nostril Breathing, an indispensable tool for anyone, particularly those within the rigorous demands of the legal profession. Tailored for practicality and effectiveness, these breathwork techniques are designed to provide swift relief and encourage long-term health and well-being amidst workplace challenges.

Alternate Nostril Breathing

Starting with a deep breath, close the right nostril with your thumb, inhale through the left nostril, then close the left nostril with your fingers, and exhale through the right nostril. The process is then reversed. This basic practice offers profound benefits for balancing the nervous system and harmonizing the two hemispheres of the brain. Alternate nostril breathing is particularly beneficial for those seeking to cultivate balance, tranquility, and mental clarity, making it an excellent technique for unwinding after a demanding day or preparing for a balanced state of mind.

To perform alternate nostril breathing, effectively it's crucial to ensure that nasal passages are clear. If you find yourself commonly struggling with nasal congestion, it may inhibit not only your ability to engage in this type of breathing but also your overall respiratory health.

For those experiencing frequent blockages, a neti pot can be a valuable tool. According to the Mayo Clinic, a neti pot uses a saltwater solution to rinse debris or mucus from the nasal cavity, which can be especially helpful for symptoms associated with nasal allergies, sinus problems, or colds. It's essential to follow directions and proper techniques in mixing the salt solution and in the application process to ensure safety and effectiveness. It is important to use distilled, sterilized, or previously boiled water.

Persistent nasal congestion may also indicate the need for a consultation with an ENT specialist or an allergist. These professionals can offer more targeted treatments or identify underlying conditions contributing to your symptoms. Remember, maintaining clear nasal passages is not only about comfort but also about facilitating better breathing practices that can significantly impact your overall well-being.

Diaphragmatic Breathing

This foundational technique focuses on engaging the diaphragm during inhalation to ensure a deep, full breath. This is the breathing technique if you just got very angry, anxious or upset about something and need to calm down. It is a great alternative to punching a wall or running to the bathroom to cry, for example. Practitioners are encouraged to place one hand on the chest and the other on the abdomen, breathing in slowly through the nose, ensuring the abdomen expands more than the chest.

This method not only facilitates core stabilization (vital for sitting or standing for extended periods) but also triggers the parasympathetic nervous system, promoting a state of calm and reducing stress levels. It's an excellent starting point for those new to breathwork, offering a straightforward practice that can be done discreetly at one's desk or during a brief moment of solitude.

Box Breathing

Also known as square breathing, this technique involves inhaling, holding the breath, exhaling, and holding again, each for an equal count of four. This method is particularly effective for enhancing focus and emotional regulation, making it suitable for moments requiring clarity and composure. Box breathing can serve as a mental reset, helping to clear the mind before important meetings or when transitioning between complex tasks.

Incorporating these breathwork techniques into the daily routine can serve as a powerful adjunct to the physical practices outlined in previous sections, such as yoga, further enhancing fascial health and stress management. Regular practice can lead to significant improvements in both physical and mental well-being, contributing to a more balanced and focused professional life.

Deepening Focus: Integrating Pratyahara And Meditation

Following the exploration of Pranayama and its profound effects on managing stress through breathing exercises, the next natural progression in our journey toward holistic health involves Pratyahara and meditation. Pratyahara, often referred to as the bridge between the body-focused practices and the mind-centric disciplines in yoga, emphasizes the withdrawal of senses from external distractions. This practice enables a deeper internalization of focus, which is essential for legal professionals who must often navigate complex and demanding environments. By learning to detach from external sensory inputs, attorneys can better manage stress and cultivate a focused mind conducive to deep, reflective thinking.

Building on the foundations laid by Pranayama and Pratyahara, meditation offers a structured approach to refining one's concentration and achieving a state of mental clarity. Through meditation, legal practitioners can enhance their cognitive functions, boost their emotional resilience, and achieve a heightened awareness crucial for effective decision-making. For those new to meditation, beginning with guided sessions available on apps or through free resources on

YouTube or podcast platforms can be beneficial. Integrating these practices supports personal well-being and enriches professional capabilities, facilitating a more thoughtful and insightful approach to legal challenges. Together, Pratyahara and meditation represent key elements in a comprehensive strategy for managing stress and elevating overall professional performance within the legal sector.

Incorporating holistic practices such as Pratyahara and meditation into daily legal work can profoundly enhance both personal well-being and professional efficacy. These practices foster an internalized state of consciousness, allowing legal professionals to focus intensely without distraction from their external environment. Similarly, Dharana, or the practice of concentration, directly supports the intense focus required for legal analysis and long hours of preparation. Dhyana, or meditation, helps deepen this focus into a profound state of contemplative insight, fostering clarity of mind that can greatly enhance strategic thinking and decision-making. Just as Pratyahara and meditation cultivate a deeper sense of internal focus and peace, they serve as metaphors for an effective legal practice by emphasizing the importance of withdrawing from external chaos to concentrate on the matters at hand.

By adopting these practices, attorneys can significantly elevate their ability to manage stress and maintain high levels of performance. Moreover, the ripple effects of such holistic health practices extend beyond individual benefits. When lawyers are physically healthier and mentally more robust, the quality of their interactions with colleagues and clients improves, promoting a more supportive and effective legal community. This collective elevation of well-being and professionalism can transform the entire profession, underscoring the profound impact of holistic health practices on legal acumen and the broader legal ecosystem.

Traditional Yet Modern Biohacks For Enhanced Fascial Health

Biohacking, a term that marries the pursuit of enhanced well-being with a tactical, experimental approach, has woven itself into the fabric of health and fitness discourse. This methodology champions a proactive stance on personal health, advocating for an intricate balance between leveraging cutting-edge scientific discoveries and honoring time-honored health practices. It encourages an individualized exploration of physiology, aiming to refine and uplift both physical and mental health through deliberate, informed intervention.

This concept gracefully bridges the gap between enduring traditional practices and the avant-garde of modern science. It embodies the synergy between millennia-old wisdom, such as the therapeutic embrace of saunas, the targeted relief provided by massage, and the holistic balance achieved through acupuncture, and the novel frontiers opened by innovations like cryotherapy, cold plunge therapy, and infrared sauna use. This melding of historical insight and contemporary breakthroughs presents a holistic paradigm for wellness, rooted in the rich soil of tradition yet reaching towards the potential of modern methodology.

Such practices, both ancient and new, serve as biohacks that directly influence fascial health. Fascia, the connective tissue that networks throughout our body, plays a pivotal role in our overall physical function and well-being. The heat from a traditional sauna session or the penetrating warmth of an infrared sauna can aid in relaxing and loosening the fascial tissue, promoting flexibility and decreasing discomfort. Similarly, the contrasting cold from cryotherapy or cold plunge therapy invigorates the body, enhancing circulation and reducing inflammation, which in turn can alleviate fascial stiffness and support recovery.

By delving into the specifics of these biohacks, we uncover the continuity in their core objectives: to detoxify, to heal, to rejuvenate, and to optimize. Each practice, whether it draws from the wisdom of our ancestors or the laboratories of today, offers a unique conduit to enhanced health. The guiding principle is a profound respect for the body's inherent capabilities, augmented by interventions that resonate with our biological rhythms and needs.

The rich tapestry of sauna traditions, from the communal banyas of Russia to the tranquil onsens of Japan and the cherished Finnish saunas, underscores a universal recognition of heat therapy's restorative powers. These traditions, though varied in execution, all contribute to the overarching narrative of biohacking for health: an acknowledgment that our bodies are capable of remarkable resilience and regeneration, given the right conditions and care.

In embracing the newfound popularity of biohacking, its roots steeped in tradition and its branches reaching into the realm of modern innovation, we find a comprehensive framework for fascial health. This approach does not discriminate between the old and the new but rather seeks to integrate the most effective elements of each. Through this exploration, we are invited to engage with our health in a way that is both deeply personal and expansively informed, leveraging the best of what has been and what is yet to come to foster a state of well-being that is as enduring as it is dynamic.

From Ancient Ritual To The Modern Sauna

The timeless tradition of sauna bathing is much more than a practice of relaxation; it's a cornerstone of holistic health strategy, especially for those in high-stress professions like law. This deep-rooted practice is now supported by research indicating its potent health benefits, particularly in mitigating the risks associated with stress-induced conditions such as cardiometabolic diseases (Henderson et al., 2021).

Legal professionals, often subjected to relentless stress, find in sauna sessions a powerful ally. The benefits extend beyond mere detoxification or muscle relaxation. The heat exposure characteristic of sauna use prompts a beneficial hormetic response at both cellular and systemic levels, enhancing the body's resilience to cardiometabolic diseases. This includes improved cardiovascular function, reduced inflammation, and a bolstering of the body's natural detoxification processes through enhanced circulation.

Moreover, the heat from sauna sessions has a direct impact on the fascial system, the connective tissue surrounding muscles and organs. Regular sauna use helps in maintaining fascial elasticity and hydration, critical for mobility and overall physical health. This aspect of sauna therapy is particularly relevant to those in high-stress occupations, where physical stagnation and the resultant fascial rigidity can be occupational hazards.

In addition to physical benefits, the mental and emotional respite offered by the sauna is invaluable. It provides a sanctuary for mental clarity and recovery, an essential counterbalance to the cognitive demands and emotional toll of legal work. This mental unwinding, facilitated by the warmth and isolation of the sauna, complements the physical benefits, enhancing overall well-being.

Adopting sauna bathing as part of a regular wellness routine is a testament to recognizing the importance of self-care in the pursuit of professional excellence and personal health. It acknowledges the profound impact of stress on both mind and body, and the necessity of proactive measures to counteract this.

The evidence backing sauna bathing as a viable intervention for health improvement among those in high-pressure roles is compelling (Henderson et al., 2021). It suggests a pathway not just to stress relief but to enhanced health and vitality, making sauna use an integral part of a holistic approach to wellness. As we seek balance in our professional and personal lives, embracing the therapeutic warmth of the sauna can play a crucial role in our overall health strategy, supporting both our fascial health and our resilience against the challenges of our environments.

Revitalizing Effects Of Cold Plunge Therapy

Cold plunge therapy, an age-old holistic practice experiencing a contemporary resurgence, invites us to explore the contrasts between the therapeutic heat of saunas and the invigorating chill of cold water immersion. This ancient tradition, now validated by modern scientific research, underscores a multifaceted approach to enhancing both physical and mental health. When we immerse ourselves in cold water, the body responds with narrowed blood vessels, focusing circulation towards essential organs. This adaptive response not only facilitates muscle recovery but also amplifies circulation upon re-warming, offering a favorite recovery technique for athletes and fitness aficionados alike.

The practice extends beyond physical recuperation, serving as a catalyst for immune system enhancement. The initial shock to the system, induced by cold water immersion, stimulates white blood cell production, bolstering the body's defense mechanisms. Moreover, it fosters mental resilience; habitual cold exposure trains the body and mind to maintain calm under duress, cultivating a mental fortitude invaluable in high-pressure scenarios. Recent studies have noted cold-water immersion's association with better mental health outcomes and shortened duration of upper respiratory tract infections, albeit emphasizing its combined benefits with breath-work for a compounded positive effect (Czarneckia et al., 2024).

Cryotherapy, embodying a modern interpretation of cold exposure, employs brief encounters with extremely cold air within a controlled setting to mirror the benefits of cold plunge therapy. This includes diminished inflammation and hastened recovery, presenting a convenient alternative for those seeking the advantages of cold exposure without the intensity of full immersion.

Comparing the therapeutic experiences offered by dry saunas and the moist heat of steam rooms reveals distinct benefits. While steam rooms, with their humid warmth, are especially beneficial for respiratory and skin health, the rigorous heat of a traditional sauna provides profound detoxification and relaxation benefits. Each modality contributes uniquely to our wellness toolkit, offering varied pathways to recovery, immunity enhancement, and overall well-being.

Integrating cold plunge therapy into our wellness regimen is more than a mere practice of physical rejuvenation; it's an engagement with a time-honored tradition that spans centuries, offering a holistic path to health. This method, especially when paired with practices like breathwork, not only supports mental well-being and fascial health but also optimizes lymphatic function, underscoring the interconnectedness of our body's systems. The resurgent popularity of cold plunge therapy speaks to a collective yearning for practices that offer holistic benefits, rooted in ancient wisdom yet profoundly relevant in today's world.

Therapeutic Power Of Massage And Fascial Health

The therapeutic power of massage extends deep into the fabric of our being, directly influencing the health of our fascia, the connective tissue that envelops muscles, organs, and nerves. The fascia's well-being is paramount for maintaining overall physical health and ensuring the smooth operation of our bodily functions. Among the myriad benefits of massage therapy, its impact on fascial health stands out, particularly in addressing the pervasive issue of spinal pain.

Exploring the therapeutic wonders of massage, especially its profound impact on fascial health, unveils a vital pathway to alleviating spinal discomfort and enhancing overall physical well-being. Myofascial massage, a specialized technique that gently stretches soft tissues and boosts muscle fiber elasticity, plays a pivotal role in this holistic approach to health. Highlighted by research, including a study that presented a noteworthy reduction in lumbo-sacral spine pain among professionally active women, this method underscores the broader benefits of massage on our body's intricate systems. By effectively reducing pain and improving tissue elasticity, myofascial massage not only fosters physical activity but also contributes significantly to the health and maintenance of fascia, ensuring our bodily structures remain harmonious and fluid (Kawa et al., 2015).

Massage therapy, thus, emerges as more than a mere avenue for relaxation; it is a critical component for sustaining the body's structural integrity. By focusing on the fascia, massage therapy helps release tension, improve blood flow, and restore mobility. The ripple effects of these benefits are far-reaching, from enhanced muscle recovery and reduced soreness to a marked decrease in stress levels.

While professional massage therapy provides these benefits directly, it's vital to recognize alternative methods for those who may not have regular access to such services. Yoga, often dubbed a 'massage from the inside out,' offers a practical and accessible way to achieve similar benefits. The stretching and poses in yoga can effectively simulate the effects of massage on the fascia, promoting flexibility, reducing tension, and improving lymphatic flow.

Different massage techniques, each with their unique focus, cater to a broad spectrum of needs, from the gentle strokes of Swedish massage aimed at relaxation to the targeted pressure of deep tissue massage for chronic tension. For athletes, sports massage provides specialized attention to overused areas, paralleling the targeted relief yoga offers through specific asanas.

Incorporating massage therapy or its alternatives into our wellness routines is not merely a luxury but a necessity for anyone committed to their long-term health and vitality. As we navigate the stresses and strains of daily life, practices like myofascial massage and yoga stand as powerful allies in our quest for physical and mental well-being, offering a path to a more balanced, pain-free existence.

Fascial Web And Meridian Harmony In Acupuncture

Acupuncture, an ancient healing practice with roots in traditional Chinese medicine, stands as a testament to the enduring power of holistic health approaches. This biohacking method, deeply intertwined with the body's energy systems and physical structures like fascia, offers a unique perspective on healing and wellness.

At the heart of acupuncture is the principle of restoring balance and harmony to the body's energies, known as Qi. According to traditional Chinese medicine, Qi flows through pathways in the body called meridians. When this flow is disrupted, it can lead to physical and emotional imbalances. Acupuncture seeks to restore this balance by inserting fine needles into specific points along the meridians, thereby stimulating the body's natural healing processes.

For those dealing with chronic or lingering injuries, acupuncture can be particularly beneficial. The practice has been shown to be effective in managing various types of pain, from acute injuries to more persistent conditions like chronic back pain or arthritis. It works not only by targeting specific pain points but also by addressing underlying imbalances that may be contributing to the discomfort.

Fascia plays a crucial role in acupuncture. Modern research suggests that acupuncture points may align with key intersections in the fascial network (Yang et al., 2015). This alignment between acupuncture points/meridians and the fascial system supports the concept that stimulating these points can affect the tension and flow within the fascial system, leading to reduced pain and improved mobility. The research underlines the interconnectedness of fascia with the body's energy pathways, providing a modern understanding of how acupuncture can influence overall fascial health and, by extension, our physical well-being.

Beyond pain relief, acupuncture is also known for its stress-reducing capabilities. The treatment promotes relaxation and can help alleviate symptoms of anxiety and depression. This aspect makes it a valuable tool for professionals who often face high-stress environments, offering a method to unwind and rebalance their mental state.

Integrating acupuncture into a wellness routine requires an open-minded approach and a willingness to explore traditional healing methods. For those new to acupuncture, starting with a few sessions to address specific concerns like pain management or stress relief can be a good introduction. It's also beneficial for individuals to communicate openly with their acupuncturist about their health goals and concerns to tailor the treatment effectively.

One of the appealing aspects of acupuncture is its

adaptability. It can be integrated with other wellness practices, such as yoga or massage, to create a comprehensive approach to health. This multifaceted strategy can enhance the overall benefits, leading to improved physical health and mental clarity.

Acupuncture stands out as a powerful ancient practice with modern relevance, especially for those seeking holistic ways to heal and maintain balance. Its ability to address both physical pain and emotional stress, coupled with its connection to the fascial system, makes it a unique and valuable component of any biohacking toolkit. Whether used as a standalone treatment or in conjunction with other wellness practices, acupuncture offers a path to enhanced well-being and harmonized body energies.

Dry Brushing And Epsom Salt Baths

In the comprehensive toolkit of self-care, dry brushing emerges as a standout practice for its simplicity and array of health benefits. This method, which involves the gentle brushing of dry skin with a soft-bristled brush, goes beyond mere surface-level effects. It is a catalyst for enhancing circulation, promoting lymphatic drainage, and rejuvenating the skin. While its historical roots are deep, the application of dry brushing in contemporary wellness routines offers a bridge to ancient wisdom through a modern lens.

Dry brushing acts on the body's largest organ, the skin, with a dual action of exfoliation and stimulation. By removing dead skin cells, it not only refines the skin's texture, making it smoother and more vibrant but also clears the way for new cell growth. The brushing motion encourages blood flow and stimulates the lymphatic system, a crucial network in our bodies responsible for eliminating toxins and waste. Unlike the cardiovascular system, with the heart at its core, the lymphatic system depends on physical movement to propel lymph fluid throughout the body. Dry brushing, therefore, serves as an external pump of sorts, invigorating this fluid movement and supporting the body's detoxification processes.

The fascia greatly benefits from the practice of dry brushing. Modern lifestyles often lead to fascial tightness, whether from prolonged sitting, repetitive motions, or the physical toll of stress. This tightness not only restricts movement but can also be a source of discomfort and chronic pain. Dry brushing gently massages the fascia, easing restrictions and fostering flexibility and fluidity in movement. This release not only improves physical mobility but also diminishes the physical manifestations of stress, contributing to a greater sense of well-being.

Incorporating Epsom salt baths into your self-care regimen enhances the benefits of dry brushing, offering a comprehensive approach to wellness that addresses both physical and emotional stress. Epsom salt, known for its high magnesium sulfate content, transforms a warm bath into a healing sanctuary that eases muscle tension, diminishes inflammation, and fosters a state of relaxation. The significance of magnesium, which is readily absorbed through the skin, extends across various bodily functions. Further, it aids in muscle and nerve operation, as well as inflammation reduction.

This practice not only augments the detoxification and relaxation initiated by dry brushing but also plays a critical role in balancing the body's mineral content, thereby amplifying its overall health and stress mitigation capabilities. The mechanical stimulation from dry brushing primes the circulatory and lymphatic systems, setting the stage for optimal absorption of Epsom salt's healing minerals during the subsequent bath.

Submerging in an Epsom salt bath after the invigorating process of dry brushing continues this journey towards relaxation and healing. The bath's warmth dilates pores, facilitating deeper penetration of magnesium and sulfate, which collectively foster muscle relaxation, reduce inflammation, and support blood circulation and oxygenation throughout the body. The presence of sulfates further promotes the health of joints, skin, and nervous tissue, thereby aiding the body's detoxification processes.

(Please note: Epsom salt baths may be contraindicated for people with diabetes, kidney disease, heart disease, or those who are pregnant. Always check with a doctor regarding the use of warm baths and Epsom salts if you have an existing medical condition.)

A recent study underscores the therapeutic potential of Epsom salt baths, particularly highlighting their beneficial effects on individuals with hypertension. Their research demonstrated that a 20-minute Neutral Immersion Bath (NIB) with Epsom salt could significantly lower Systolic Blood Pressure (SBP) and alter heart rate variability (HRV), indicating a reduction in sympathetic nervous system activity with an increase in parasympathetic dominance. This physiological shift suggests that Epsom salt baths are not only effective for relaxation and detoxification but also offer profound benefits for cardiovascular health, thereby making them an integral component of managing hypertension (Joicy et al., 2021).

Following the Epsom salt bath, it's advisable to allow your

body a period of rest to fully assimilate the benefits, optimizing detoxification and mineral uptake. To maintain the integrity of the skin's natural oils and the newly absorbed minerals, it's recommended to forego the use of soap during the bath, thus ensuring the therapeutic effects continue to work long after you've stepped out of the water.

By blending the mechanical benefits of dry brushing with the mineral-rich properties of Epsom salt baths, we harness a powerful duo in the fight against stress and inflammation. This holistic strategy not only elevates the physical and emotional relaxation initiated by dry brushing but also fortifies the body's mineral balance, supporting a comprehensive wellness regime.

Concluding your bath with the application of a natural moisturizer or oil is key to locking in hydration and soothing the skin. This step is not only about surface-level care but also supports the fascia's health by maintaining its hydration and elasticity. Products rich in natural ingredients like shea butter, coconut oil, or jojoba oil not only nourish the skin but also offer additional health benefits.

Creating a spa-like environment at home, complete with calming scents, soft lighting, and soothing sounds, significantly enhances this wellness practice. You can also use this time to listen to motivating or inspiring audio books or music. Such an atmosphere boosts the sensory experience, transforming each self-care session into a holistic ritual that rejuvenates the body, calms the mind, and uplifts the spirit.

In this sanctuary of tranquility, it's crucial to address the common, yet misleading, allure of pairing a hot bath with alcohol. The image of unwinding in warm waters with a glass of wine may seem appealing but is ultimately counterproductive to the goals of relaxation and health. Alcohol consumption, especially in the context of a relaxing Epsom salt bath, can disrupt sleep patterns, lead to dehydration, and foster a false sense of relaxation that often results in increased anxiety. These effects directly contradict the therapeutic intentions behind such a wellness ritual. For a more beneficial experience, consider sipping on a warm cup of herbal tea or a refreshing, healthy beverage. These alternatives not only hydrate the body and enhance the detoxifying properties of the bath but also contribute to genuine relaxation and well-being without the adverse effects of alcohol.

This holistic approach to fascial wellness which incorporates the tangible benefits of dry brushing and Epsom salt baths with the mental and emotional clarity fostered by a carefully curated environment, stands as a powerful strategy for navigating the pressures of professional life. It embodies the time-honored understanding that our physical health is inextricably linked to our emotional state, guiding us toward a life that is not only balanced but deeply fulfilling.

Reconsidering Personal Care Products

The beauty and cosmetics industry, while often associated with enhancing personal appearance and confidence, harbors a deeper concern related to the health implications of its products. This issue transcends gender, affecting not only those who use makeup but also individuals using men's grooming products such as soap, deodorant, shaving lotions and aftershaves. A critical point of concern centers on the presence of phthalates, a class of chemicals found in numerous beauty and personal care items.

The incorporation of these chemicals into everyday products raises important questions about their long-term impact on the body, particularly concerning the fascial and lymphatic systems. Phthalates and other similar chemicals have the potential to disrupt these critical systems, contributing to a buildup of toxins and interfering with the body's natural regulatory processes.

Such disruptions can lead to inflammation, a key factor in a range of health issues, and potentially compromise the body's ability to maintain its delicate balance of cleansing and renewal. Given the fascial and lymphatic systems' roles in detoxification and protecting against disease, understanding and mitigating the effects of harmful chemicals found in personal care products become imperative for maintaining holistic health and well-being (Barrett, 2005).

The dialogue around beauty products and their ingredients isn't intended to create fear but to foster awareness and informed choices. The truth is, genuine beauty and well-being stem from healthy habits and self-care practices that support the body's natural vitality. The reliance on external products for beauty enhancement overlooks the foundational elements of true radiance, such as a nutritious diet, adequate hydration, and a balanced lifestyle. All of these factors play a crucial role in maintaining the health and flexibility of our fascia, reinforcing the connection between our skincare choices and our overall physical health.

For individuals seeking to navigate the complex landscape of personal care products, there are steps to minimize exposure to potentially harmful chemicals. Transitioning to natural and organic beauty and grooming products offers a viable alternative, reducing the risk associated with synthetic ingredients. These products, often formulated from plant-based sources, provide the desired aesthetic benefits without compromising health. By choosing products that are kind to our fascia, we not only enhance our external appearance but also support our body's intricate network of connective tissue.

Moreover, embracing a more minimalist approach to beauty and grooming can further reduce chemical exposure. Simplifying routines by selecting products with fewer ingredients or using them less frequently can have a profound impact on reducing the body's chemical load. It's about striking a balance between enhancing one's appearance and prioritizing overall health and well-being. This approach aligns with the principle of caring for the fascia by avoiding substances that can lead to inflammation or tightness, promoting a state of physical wellness that reflects in our appearance.

Creating a healthier relationship with beauty and grooming products also involves recognizing the power of marketing and the allure of quick fixes. The promise of instant transformation through a product can be tempting, but true beauty and health are cultivated from within through consistent care and mindful choices. It's about enhancing, not masking, one's natural appearance and embracing practices that nourish both the body and spirit. In doing so, we not only take care of our fascial health but also foster a genuine sense of beauty that radiates from within.

Navigating the world of beauty and grooming products with a health-conscious mindset does not require abandoning these rituals altogether. Instead, it's about making thoughtful choices, seeking out safer alternatives, and understanding the profound connection between personal care practices and overall health. By adopting a more informed and holistic approach to beauty and grooming, individuals can enjoy the benefits of these products while safeguarding their health and well-being, regardless of gender. This view extends to the care of our fascia, emphasizing that true beauty can be a reflection of our internal well-being.

Understanding and caring for our fascial health emerges as a pivotal component of holistic wellness, particularly for those navigating high-stress professions like law. The interconnectedness of fascia with our physical, emotional, and even spiritual well-being underscores its significance beyond mere structural support. By nurturing our fascial health through movement, hydration, therapeutic treatments, and mindful practices, we not only alleviate physical discomforts but also liberate stored stress and emotional burdens. This holistic approach not only enhances our physical resilience but also sharpens our mental acuity and emotional clarity, equipping us to thrive both personally and professionally. Embracing fascial care thus becomes not just a health strategy but a transformative journey towards greater balance, vitality, and sustainable success in our legal endeavors and beyond.

Chapter 4: Sleep Like Your Brain Depends On It

Embracing sleep as a pillar of health is not merely a choice but a necessity, especially when considering its profound impact on our brain function. Sleep, often sacrificed at the altar of productivity, is actually the cornerstone upon which mental clarity, emotional resilience, and physical vitality rest. Far from being a mere period of rest, sleep is an active, vital process that intertwines with every aspect of our physiology, deeply influencing our cognitive functions, mood regulation, and overall well-being.

A study highlights the critical functions of sleep, emphasizing its necessity for waking cognition, attention sustainability, and even survival. This research shows that cognitive performance and vigilant attention begin to wane after more than 16 hours of wakefulness, underscoring the importance of not just the quantity but the quality of sleep. The study further reveals that sleep deficits from partial deprivation can accumulate over time, resulting in a steady deterioration of alertness and cognitive performance (Worley, 2018).

We all need to value achieving consistent, quality sleep patterns free from disturbances. The consequences of neglecting this are far from trivial; inadequate sleep is linked to a cascade of negative outcomes, including diminished cognitive functions, deteriorating mental health, and an increased risk of accidents.

This exploration is more than an academic exercise; it's a call to action to prioritize sleep in our lives. By understanding the significant roles sleep plays in our mental and physical health, we can begin to implement strategies to cultivate a conducive sleep environment. From challenging prevalent myths about sleep aids to adjusting daily routines that undermine restful nights, this journey is about recognizing sleep as a fundamental necessity for a vibrant, energetic, and fulfilling existence.

Moreover, integrating the insights from the study, this section encourages a reevaluation of our sleep habits, understanding that securing consolidated sleep, characterized by appropriate non-REM and REM sequences, is crucial for its restorative benefits. Achieving sleep that aligns with our circadian rhythms further enhances its effectiveness, ensuring we wake up rejuvenated and ready to tackle the demands of the day.

Understanding And Overcoming Sleep Challenges

In a competitive industry, the concept of being a short sleeper, or someone who claims to function optimally on minimal sleep, is often worn as a badge of honor. However, this section aims to debunk this myth and address other common misconceptions about sleep needs. It will also provide tools and techniques for tracking and improving sleep quality, as well as strategies for increasing sleep duration and efficiency.

The notion that some people can function optimally on just 4-5 hours of sleep per night is a pervasive myth. While it's true that individual sleep needs can vary, the vast majority of adults require between 7-9 hours of sleep for optimal health and cognitive function. Chronic sleep deprivation, even if you feel you're coping well, can lead to serious long-term health consequences, including increased risk of cardiovascular disease, obesity, diabetes, and cognitive decline. For attorneys, whose work requires sharp thinking, attention to detail, and emotional regulation, skimping on sleep can significantly impair performance and judgment.

Understanding your sleep patterns is the first step toward improving sleep quality. Tools like sleep trackers can provide insights into your sleep duration, disturbances, and cycles. While these devices aren't always perfectly accurate, they can offer a helpful overview of your sleep patterns and highlight areas for improvement. Techniques such as maintaining a sleep diary can also be beneficial. By recording bedtime, wake-up time, quality of sleep, and any disturbances, you can start to identify patterns and triggers that affect your sleep. If you wear any type of smartwatch, you may already have a sleep diary recorded, or can start one easily.

For those accustomed to short sleep durations, suddenly aiming for 8 hours a night can be daunting and unrealistic. Instead, try gradually increasing your sleep time by going to bed 15-20 minutes earlier each night until you reach the desired duration. It's also crucial to create a conducive sleep environment and establish a relaxing bedtime routine. Dimming the lights, lowering the temperature, and engaging in calming activities like reading or meditation can signal to your body that it's time to wind down.

Sleep efficiency refers to the percentage of time you spend in bed actually sleeping. Improving sleep efficiency involves not just increasing sleep duration but making sure that the sleep you're getting is restful and uninterrupted. Strategies to improve sleep efficiency include sticking to a consistent sleep schedule, even on weekends; creating a bedtime routine that signals to your body it's time to sleep; and optimizing your sleep environment for comfort and relaxation. Avoiding caffeine and heavy meals before bedtime, as well as reducing exposure to screens and blue light in the evening, can also help improve sleep quality.

Interconnectivity Of Sleep And Health

For legal professionals, whose days are often filled with complex problem-solving, rigorous analysis, and high-stakes decision-making, understanding the science of sleep and its profound impact on health is not just beneficial but essential. Sleep isn't merely a period of rest; it's an active, dynamic process during which the body and brain undergo critical repair, rejuvenation, and consolidation.

Sleep is structured in cycles, each comprising different stages that serve specific functions. These cycles repeat several times throughout the night. The two primary types of sleep are Rapid Eye Movement (REM) sleep and Non-REM sleep, which is further divided into three stages. Non-REM sleep is when most of the deep, restorative sleep occurs. During these stages, the body repairs muscles and tissues, stimulates growth and development, boosts immune function, and builds up energy for the next day. REM sleep, on the other hand, is when most dreaming occurs and is essential for cognitive functions like memory consolidation, learning, and emotional processing. For legal professionals, this means that cutting sleep short can significantly impact their ability to think clearly, remember important details, and manage their emotions effectively.

Adequate sleep is paramount for maintaining and enhancing brain health. During sleep, especially during the deep stages of Non-REM sleep, the brain is busy repairing and regenerating neural networks. It's also consolidating memories from the day, making sense of the vast amount of information absorbed, and embedding the skills learned. This process is crucial for legal professionals who constantly engage in complex thinking and learning. Moreover, sleep helps clear the brain of waste products that can potentially contribute to neurodegenerative diseases. Without enough quality sleep, cognitive functions such as judgment, problem-solving, and attention to detail can suffer, all of which are critical in the legal field.

Incorporating insights from recent research underscores the broader impacts of sleep on health beyond cognitive functions (Grandner 2017). Insufficient sleep duration and poor sleep quality have been linked to an increased risk of mortality, with both very short and very long sleep durations associated with higher mortality rates. This highlights the critical need for balanced sleep patterns, as extremes in sleep duration can be detrimental to health.

Furthermore, sleep deficiency has been associated with several serious health issues including obesity, diabetes, cardiovascular disease, and inflammation. These conditions are of particular concern for professionals like lawyers, who often endure the pressures of sedentary lifestyles compounded by high stress. Establishing regular, healthy sleep patterns can help mitigate these risks and promote a healthier, more balanced lifestyle.

The legal profession is inherently stressful, and chronic stress can significantly impact both physical and mental health. Sleep serves as a powerful countermeasure to stress, regulating stress-related hormones such as cortisol and supporting emotional regulation. Adequate sleep enhances mood, improves anxiety management, and bolsters overall emotional resilience. Prioritizing sleep is not merely an investment in physical and cognitive health; it equips legal professionals with the emotional strength needed to navigate the challenges of their demanding careers.

For people whose minds are constantly engaged in analytical thinking, sleep is not just a luxury; it's a crucial element of functioning at one's best. Cultivating the perfect sleep environment is about transforming your bedroom into a sanctuary that invites rest and rejuvenation. Create a sleep haven that mirrors the tranquility and comfort of a luxury hotel suite while emphasizing the importance of darkness, quality bedding, and the right pillows for optimal sleep.

Imagine stepping into a luxury hotel suite at the end of a long day. What makes it so inviting? It's the serene atmosphere, the tasteful decor, and the unmistakable sense of being a place dedicated to rest. Your bedroom should be no different. Start by removing all clutter and distractions. Choose calming colors for your walls and bedding, and consider adding elements like plants or artwork that induce a sense of peace. The goal is to create an environment that signals to your body and mind that it's time to unwind and rest.

Our bodies are governed by a circadian rhythm, an internal clock that cues us to feel awake or sleepy in response to external light signals. When light enters the eyes, it signals the brain to halt the production of melatonin, the hormone responsible for sleep. This is perfectly natural during the day, but at night, even the smallest amount of light can disrupt this cycle. Blackout curtains create a pitch-black environment, shielding your sleep from streetlights, car headlights, and even the early morning sun. This darkness helps maintain your body's natural rhythm, allowing for a deeper and more restorative sleep.

Even if you're able to fall asleep in a lit room, the quality of that sleep might be compromised. Light exposure during sleep can lead to more frequent awakenings and a shift from deep REM sleep to the lighter stages of sleep. This can leave you feeling groggy and unrefreshed in the morning, even after a full night's rest. By ensuring complete darkness, blackout curtains can improve not only the duration but also the quality of your sleep, helping you wake up feeling more alert and refreshed. For those living in urban areas with bright night-time lighting, or for rooms facing east where the early morning sun is particularly potent, they are an indispensable tool in maintaining a sleep-friendly environment year-round.

Beyond their practical function, blackout curtains also contribute to creating a tranquil and calming sleep environment. They can serve as a physical barrier, separating your busy, stress-filled work life from the peaceful retreat of your bedroom. This psychological distinction is crucial for professionals who often bring work home. When you draw the curtains, it's a signal to your mind that the day is done, and it's time to shift into a state of relaxation and rest.

The bedding you choose plays a significant role in your comfort and, consequently, your ability to sleep well. Good quality, organic sheets are a worthwhile investment. They're not only kinder to your skin but also to the environment. While high thread count is often equated with luxury, it's not the only indicator of quality. Look for sheets made from natural fibers like cotton, bamboo, or linen, which are breathable and can help regulate your body temperature throughout the night.

Remember, the most expensive option isn't always the best. Focus on feel and comfort to suit your personal preferences.

Your pillow is more than just a soft place to rest your head; it's a crucial support for your neck and spine. Choosing the right pillow can mean the difference between waking up refreshed and suffering from neck pain or headaches. Consider your typical sleep position: side sleepers may need a thicker pillow to keep their head aligned with their spine, while stomach sleepers might benefit from a softer, flatter pillow. Memory foam, feather, or latex pillows all have different qualities, so take the time to find one that supports you best. Additionally, support cushions like knee or body pillows can further aid in maintaining proper alignment and ensuring a comfortable night's sleep.

Creating the perfect sleep environment is an investment in your health and well-being, particularly crucial for those in the legal profession. By transforming your bedroom into a sanctuary, ensuring complete darkness, choosing the right bedding, and selecting supportive pillows, you're setting the stage for a restful and rejuvenating sleep. This isn't just about aesthetics; it's about creating a space that supports your physical and mental recovery, ensuring you're at your best during the waking hours.

Chapter 5: Nutrition To Fuel Body And Mind

In an era where our diets are increasingly influenced by a flood of nutritional misinformation and the allure of convenience, discerning the path to true health has become more challenging than ever. For professionals like attorneys, who operate in high-stress environments and rely heavily on their mental acuity and physical stamina, understanding how to navigate through a landscape saturated with addictive food choices is essential to vitality. This chapter isn't about prescribing a strict diet; it's about arming you with the knowledge and tools to make informed, healthy food choices.

Recent research has shed light on the pervasive impact of ultra-processed foods (UPFs) on global health. A revolution in food science and modern grocery retailing over the past 60 years has led to an explosive growth in the consumption of UPFs. These aren't just foods that have been modified by processing; they are formulations of low-cost substances derived from food, with little to no whole foods, often containing additives that heighten their appeal and durability.

Designed for maximum profit, they are hyper-palatable, highly branded, and aggressively marketed. Yet, their consumption is significantly associated with an array of adverse health outcomes, from obesity and type 2 diabetes to cardiovascular diseases and even all-cause mortality. The evidence is clear: UPFs are a substantial factor affecting worldwide increases in the prevalence of diet-related non-communicable diseases (UNC Global Food Research Program, 2021).

We must stop falling for the deceptive allure of ultra-processed foods and unveil the truth behind their impact on our health. We need to stop deceiving ourselves by marketing that assures us eating cheap fast food is justified because it's convenient. We'll delve into the science that reveals the detrimental effects of a UPF-dominated diet and offer strategies for gradually eliminating these harmful substances from your meals. It's about understanding that every choice you make at the dining table is a choice for your future health and well-being.

If your days are filled with making critical decisions and having to think on your feet, the food you consume plays a vital role in fueling those decisions. It's time to apply the same level of scrutiny and care to your diet as you do to your professional work. By committing to informed and healthier food choices, you're not just enhancing your physical health; you're setting the stage for sustained mental performance and focus. This journey is about transformation, not deprivation or restriction.

The Harsh Reality Of Ultra-Processed Foods

In our fast-paced, convenience-driven world, the food landscape is increasingly dominated by ultra-processed foods (UPFs), presenting a significant challenge to our health. These foods, while convenient and tantalizing in taste, contribute to a range of detrimental health outcomes. Emerging research underscores the concerning link between high consumption of UPFs and an elevated risk of non-communicable diseases (NCDs), obesity, cardiovascular diseases, cerebrovascular disease, depression, and even all-cause mortality (Pagliai et al., 2021). This trend underscores the urgency with which individuals dedicated to excellence in all areas of life must recognize and mitigate the impact of these foods.

The notion that ultra-processed foods (UPFs) are merely benign, empty calories underestimates their true danger. In reality, they pose a significant threat to our health, particularly due to the added sugars they contain, which are not merely void of nutrition but actively trigger harmful biochemical reactions. These reactions can lead to metabolic diseases, drawing us into a cycle of cravings and health decline. The allure of these foods, compounded by their design to be irresistible, results in consumption levels beyond what our bodies can healthily manage. This leads to metabolic dysfunctions, with fructose's impact on liver metabolism being notably similar to alcohol, causing conditions like fatty liver disease and insulin resistance, which are precursors to a wide array of health issues.

This situation is exacerbated by the food industry's strategic addition of sugar to UPFs, not just for taste, but for its addictive properties, making the avoidance of these foods a considerable challenge for the average consumer. This insidious strategy contributes to the increased prevalence of non-communicable diseases such as obesity, diabetes, cardiovascular diseases, and even cancer, marking UPFs as not just unhealthy but genuinely toxic and addictive components of our diet. The systemic issue of UPFs in our diet necessitates not only informed personal dietary choices but also broader regulatory interventions to mitigate the consumption of these harmful substances (Lustig, 2020).

In understanding the severe implications of UPFs and taking deliberate steps to reduce their presence in our diets, we safeguard our health and well-being. This commitment to health, especially for professionals who demand excellence in every aspect of their lives, means making educated, healthier dietary choices that support long-term vitality and performance. As we aim for success in our careers, integrating a conscientious approach to our diet becomes crucial, highlighting the need to reject these harmful foods actively.

The misperception of healthfulness surrounding certain UPFs arises from clever marketing strategies, with labels boasting terms like "all-natural," "low-fat," "fortified," "gluten-free," and even "organic." However, these claims do not necessarily equate to a product being wholesome or nutritious. Below is an expanded list of commonly misconstrued "healthy" UPFs, illustrating the breadth of the issue:

1. **Chips, Crackers, and "Whole Grain" Snacks:** Despite claims of whole grains, these are typically high in sodium, artificial flavors, refined oils, and preservatives.

2. **Protein Bars:** Often packed with sugars, syrups, and highly processed protein isolates, masquerading as a healthful choice.

3. **Boxed Cereals and Granola:** Marketed for benefits like weight loss or heart health yet loaded with cheap, highly processed grains and excess sugars while being low in fiber.

4. **Boxed Rice, Pasta Dishes, and Instant Noodles:** These convenient meals are full of sodium, artificial additives, and lack substantial nutritional value. Some varieties are pre-fried in refined hydrogenated oils.

5. **Pre-made Smoothies and Juice Drinks:** These can contain as much sugar as sodas. Homemade alternatives allow for better control over ingredients.

6. **Frozen Foods for Air Fryers:** Typically pre-fried in unhealthy oils and highly processed, these items offer little beyond convenience.

7. **"Low-Fat" and "Fat-Free" Products:** Often contain added sugars and artificial thickeners to replace the flavor

and texture lost when fat is removed.

8. **Vegetable Chips:** Might seem healthier than traditional potato chips, but are typically deep fried and often include unnecessary sugars and artificial coloring.

9. **Store-Bought Salad Dressings and Sauces:** High in preservatives, sodium, sugars, and processed oils, which can negate the health benefits of a fresh salad.

10. **Meat Alternatives:** The surge in vegan and vegetarian options has led to an increase in UPFs that mimic meat, often compromising nutritional value for taste and texture.

11. **Sweetened Yogurts and Dairy Alternatives:** Commonly loaded with added sugars. Opt for plain versions of yogurt without added sugar (add fresh or frozen fruit.)

This list underscores a critical message: the healthiest foods are usually those that undergo minimal processing. These foods retain their natural nutrients, including vitamins, minerals, fibers, and antioxidants, all essential for maintaining optimal health and supporting the intricate network of our fascia.

Adopting a diet centered around whole foods means prioritizing fresh produce, lean meats and fish if you eat animal products, tofu, beans, whole grains, nuts, and seeds. We all know the adage about the most wholesome foods are primarily found along the perimeter of the grocery store. For those able to invest in organic options, such choices can further reduce exposure to pesticides and chemicals. However, it's essential to remember that incorporating any whole foods into your diet, whether organic or not, represents a significant step toward minimizing UPF consumption.

It's a fundamental truth that often goes overlooked: we are, quite literally, built from what we eat. Every cell in our body, every fiber of our being, is constructed from the nutrients (or lack thereof) that we derive from our meals. This profound connection between our diet and our physical form underscores the critical importance of prioritizing food quality over mere caloric intake or cost savings.

Transitioning from this foundational understanding, it's crucial to challenge the prevailing attitude that prioritizes cost-saving over nutritional richness. This common yet misguided belief not only undermines the essence of true nourishment but also harbors potential detriment to our well-being. It cultivates a notion where quantity is mistakenly celebrated over the quality of our dietary choices, suggesting that financial frugality can justify a compromise in nutritional integrity. Yet, such a narrow view overlooks a vital aspect: allocating resources towards premium-quality food is a profound investment in our health and longevity, a strategic choice that pays dividends in vitality and overall life quality. The short-term savings achieved by opting for lower-priced, processed options pale in comparison to the prospective healthcare costs and diminished life quality that may ensue, making the case for prioritizing high-quality nutrition indisputable.

Understanding budgetary constraints are real and affect choices, particularly when you have a family to feed, it's crucial to navigate these limitations with a strategy that still prioritizes nutrient density and food quality. This might mean adjusting other areas of spending to ensure your diet doesn't suffer or finding creative ways to incorporate whole foods into your meals without breaking the bank. Moreover, when we choose to invest in better-quality foods, such as opting for organic produce and grass-fed meats, we're not just benefiting our bodies. We're also supporting more sustainable and ethical farming practices, contributing to a healthier planet alongside our healthier selves.

The modern diet's increasing reliance on UPFs is more than a nutritional concern; it's a psychological battle akin to addiction. This is not a pseudo-addiction to food in general, as it is specific to UPFs. The designed allure of these foods, with their high contents of sugars, fats, and artificial additives, triggers the brain's reward pathways, leading to patterns of compulsive eating that parallel substance abuse disorders (Lustig 2020). The deceptive marketing of UPFs, often adorned with health claims, masks their potential for dependency and health risks, misleading consumers seeking better dietary choices.

The acknowledgment of the addictive qualities of UPFs opens the door to exploring avenues for intervention and recovery. Beyond individual efforts to choose whole foods, there's a growing need for societal and policy-level actions that make healthier options accessible and appealing while limiting the reach of UPFs (Lustig, 2020). Education plays a pivotal role, empowering consumers to discern between genuinely nutritious foods and those that only offer fleeting satisfaction at the expense of long-term health.

Addressing food disorders and addictions require a compassionate, comprehensive approach that recognizes the biological, psychological, and social factors at play (Lustig, 2020). Support systems, whether through healthcare providers, community programs, or online forums, can offer guidance and encouragement for those looking to break free from the grip of UPFs. The journey toward overcoming food challenges isn't just about dietary changes; it's about reclaiming control over one's health and well-being, fostering a lifestyle that prioritizes nourishment, balance, and true satisfaction.

While the pull of UPFs in the modern world is undeniable,

understanding their impact on our health and recognizing the patterns of addiction they can foster are crucial steps toward making informed dietary choices. By prioritizing whole, minimally processed foods and advocating for broader access to healthy options, individuals and communities can counteract the lure of UPFs, fostering a culture of wellness that supports physical, mental, and emotional health.

The Particular Dangers Of Highly-Processed Seed Oils

Transitioning from the broader category of Ultra-Processed Foods (UPFs) to a specific, yet significantly harmful sub-category, we delve into the realm of highly-processed seed oils. Found abundantly in commercial snacks, baked goods, fried foods, and numerous fast-food dishes, these oils warrant a focused discussion due to their profound health implications. Particularly concerning is the frequent use of such oils subjected to repeated heating, as observed in fast-food fryers, posing significant health risks. This concern is not merely anecdotal but supported by scientific consensus, highlighting the urgent need for professionals and individuals alike to acknowledge and mitigate these risks.

Highly-processed seed oils such as canola, corn, cottonseed, soy, sunflower, safflower, grape seed, and rice bran, collectively dubbed the "Hateful 8" by Dr. Cate Shanahan, have been linked to detrimental effects on metabolic health, exacerbating inflammation and compromising immune function (Shanahan, 2024.) They are often labeled with the healthy-sounding euphemism "vegetable oil."

Scientific research reveals that when oils undergo repeated

heating, their chemical structure undergoes significant changes. Repeatedly heated oils exhibit higher peroxide values compared to unheated or singly heated oils, indicating increased oxidative degradation. This degradation results in the production of harmful free radicals, which contribute to oxidative stress and subsequent cellular and molecular damage (Ambreen, Siddiq, & Hussain, 2020).

The consumption of repeatedly reheated oil and highly-processed seed oils is closely associated with inflammation, a precursor to various chronic diseases. Studies demonstrate the impact of long-term consumption of oxidized mixed vegetable oils on liver function, showing significant hepatic damage through fat accumulation and oxidative stress. Even low doses of thermally oxidized oils can impair liver function (Ambreen, Siddiq, & Hussain, 2020).

Recognizing the dangers associated with highly-processed seed oils necessitates a paradigm shift, viewing foods cooked in these oils not as occasional indulgences but as significant contributors to systemic inflammation and related health problems. Opting for higher-quality oils or whole foods represents a healthier choice and a step towards redefining what a treat truly means, focusing on nourishment over transient pleasure.

This awareness underscores the importance of informed dietary decisions, especially for individuals in demanding careers. Transitioning to a diet rich in whole foods and healthier oils mitigates the risks associated with highly-processed seed oils, promoting overall well-being and enabling peak performance. By prioritizing metabolic health through dietary choices, legal professionals can enhance their resilience and well-being, ensuring they are better equipped to navigate the rigorous demands of their profession while safeguarding their long-term health.

Raising Your Standards: Indulging Mindfully

In the pursuit of health, the mantra of 'quality over quantity' becomes not just a guiding principle but a way of life. Professionals trying to improve their health and lives must redefine indulgence, shifting the focus from mindless consumption to a thoughtful celebration of food. It's about understanding that occasional treats are not just permissible but can be an integral part of a balanced and joyful life, provided these occasional treats are of high quality.

There's a world of difference between a store-bought, mass-produced sweets laden with preservatives and a homemade dessert crafted with care and top-quality ingredients. The former is designed for a long shelf life. Think of the "treats" that can sit on shelves in your pantry for weeks, months and even years that would still taste the same if you ate them. The latter, however, is an act of love and artistry. Real homemade treats and baked goods go stale and grow mold quickly, as they do not have the chemical preservatives and stabilizing highly-processed oils of commercial baked goods.

Healthy indulgence is about savoring flavors, appreciating the craftsmanship, and acknowledging the effort that goes into creating something truly special. When you do choose to indulge, make it count. Opt for that slice of homemade pie, that artisanal chocolate, or that delicacy from a bakery that prioritizes quality. These are not just treats; they're experiences, and they should be enjoyed to the fullest.

While the occasional high-quality treat can be enjoyed as part of a balanced diet, the habitual consumption of low-quality, ultra processed foods containing refined oils poses significant health risks. These items, often high in added sugars, unhealthy fats, and artificial additives, contribute little to your nutritional needs while increasing the risk of various health issues, including obesity, diabetes, and heart disease. It's the daily, mindless consumption of these foods that is most damaging. It's a pattern that not only harms your physical health but also dulls your palate and diminishes your ability to enjoy and appreciate the subtleties and complexities of well-prepared food.

We need to stop mindlessly eating highly-processed baked goods as daily indulgences. Enjoy the occasional treat, and when you do, make it count. Adopting a quality over quantity approach to indulgence is a powerful strategy for enhancing your health and enriching your culinary experiences. It's about raising your standards. As you continue to navigate the demands of your professional and personal life, let this principle guide your food choices, leading you toward a path of better health, greater enjoyment, and a deeper appreciation for the food you eat.

The Transformative Power Of Removing Harmful Foods

The first step in health transformation is to understand the detrimental effects of UPFs and to minimize or completely eliminate their intake. These substances have a pervasive influence on our well-being, weight management, and overall quality of life. The transformative power of cutting out these harmful foods is profound and multifaceted, offering not just physical benefits but also significant mental and emotional improvements.

Sugar, particularly when refined, is not merely a sweetening agent but a potent substance capable of inciting a myriad of health complications when consumed excessively. Its adverse effects span from obesity and type 2 diabetes to heart disease and specific cancers. Similarly, highly processed carbohydrates, swiftly metabolized into sugars, wreak havoc on the body's glycemic balance. They precipitate sharp increases in blood glucose and insulin levels, ushering in a vicious cycle of cravings, overconsumption, and ensuing health detriments. While individuals with physically demanding professions or athletes might metabolize these carbohydrates more efficiently due to their higher energy expenditures, the reality for those with more sedentary lifestyles, particularly office workers spending prolonged hours seated, is starkly different. For the latter group, the long-term consumption of such foods poses significant health risks, underscoring the necessity for dietary mindfulness and moderation.

Cutting out or significantly reducing sugar and highly processed carbohydrates from your diet can lead to remarkable health improvements. Weight management becomes more straightforward as the body shifts from storing fat to burning it. Energy levels stabilize, no longer subject to the highs and lows of sugar spikes and crashes. Mental clarity, mood stability, and overall cognitive function also improve, making this change not just a physical transformation but a mental and emotional one as well.

Cravings for sugar and processed carbohydrates are often not just about physical hunger; they're about habits and emotional needs. These cravings can be powerful, but they are not insurmountable. Understanding that these desires are often a response to stress, emotional voids, or habit rather than genuine nutritional needs is crucial. By recognizing and addressing the underlying triggers, individuals can start to break the cycle of addiction to these substances. Replacing harmful foods with nourishing alternatives isn't about deprivation; it's about retraining the palate and the mind to enjoy and crave foods that truly nourish and sustain.

As you begin to replace harmful foods with healthier alternatives, the changes go beyond just physical health. Many report a sense of empowerment and control over their choices and lives. There's a newfound appreciation for the flavors and textures of whole, minimally processed foods. Mood and energy levels stabilize, leading to better performance and satisfaction in both personal and professional realms. The journey might be challenging initially, but the rewards are worth the effort.

Sugar and highly processed carbohydrates might be ubiquitous and seemingly indispensable in our convenience-driven world, but the benefits of reducing their consumption are clear and compelling. As we strive towards excellence, making this change is not just about improving physical health; it's about setting a foundation for sustained performance, mental clarity, and overall well-being. The transformative power of cutting out harmful foods is a testament to the incredible ability of our bodies and minds to heal and thrive when given the right nourishment.

Approaching Nutrition As A Case For Trial

For most lawyers in their professions, your every action is strategic, every hour billed, and every case meticulously planned. It's this level of dedication that secures victories and cements reputations. Yet, when it comes to the most fundamental aspect of life, your nutrition and how it affects your health, the strategy often falls by the wayside. It's a disconnect that doesn't align with the rest of your highly structured life. This section is not a set of rules or a diet plan; it's a call to integrate the same level of care and strategy into your eating habits as you do in your professional life.

You've built a career on understanding the nuances, predicting outcomes, and navigating complex negotiations. Now, apply that foresight to your health. When you're preparing for a long day, do you fuel yourself with the equivalent of fast, empty words, or do you nourish your mind and body with substance that will sustain and support you through hours of concentration? Just as you wouldn't walk into a negotiation without preparation, don't approach your meals without the same consideration.

Every successful case is backed by hours of preparation, research, and strategy. Your diet deserves the same attention. Dedicate time each week, not as an afterthought but as a scheduled, non-negotiable appointment, to plan your meals. This isn't about complex recipes or hours in the kitchen; it's about thoughtful, strategic choices. What will give you the most sustained energy? What will keep your mind sharp? Just as you'd choose the right expert witness or study jury behavior, choose foods that will best support your body and mind through the trials of your day. These days, there's also an incredible amount of healthy meal choices for busy professionals. If you truly have zero time to cook or plan meals, consider these services to get your nutrition on track.

Your meals should be as deliberate and purposeful as your work. This might mean preparing a week's worth of lunches in advance or simply deciding on a healthy take-out option. Whatever the strategy, it should be intentional, not reactive. After all, you wouldn't walk into a courtroom unprepared; don't let your meals be an afterthought.

Eating proper nutrition for health isn't about a diet or following a trend. It's about recognizing that the care, strategy, and dedication you apply to your work should also be reflected in how you fuel your body and mind. It's about making choices that align with your values, goals, and the high standards you set for every other aspect of your life. You are your most valuable asset, and it's time to invest in yourself with the same rigor and commitment you apply to your profession.

Compassion And Understanding In Dietary Changes

Embarking on a journey to alter eating habits, particularly in shifting away from UPFs towards a whole food-centric diet, transcends individual effort; it is an inclusive mission that extends to the workplace as much as it does within a family setting. Achieving a healthier lifestyle demands not only personal dedication but also the creation of a supportive atmosphere by those around us, including co-workers and office staff, whose resistance or objections to dietary changes can pose additional hurdles.

Approaching dietary transformation necessitates patience, self-compassion, and an understanding that change unfolds gradually, often with setbacks. It's about prioritizing progress over perfection and appreciating the effort required for even the smallest steps forward. This mindset is crucial when dealing with the challenges posed by UPFs, which may exhibit addictive properties akin to those of substance use disorders (Gearhardt et al., 2023). Recognizing personal struggles with UPF addiction or unhealthy eating habits is a critical move toward positive change.

The journey toward a healthier diet involves identifying personal challenges linked to UPF addiction or unhealthy eating patterns, emphasizing the importance of securing appropriate support. This can take the form of professional advice, community groups, or resources dedicated to fostering healthier lifestyles. Within the professional realm, this may also involve initiating health and wellness dialogues, advocating for healthier food choices during meetings, and sharing supportive resources with colleagues.

Transitioning dietary habits within a household or office necessitates open communication and a collective approach. It's about articulating the value of these changes to family members or colleagues and exploring mutual benefits. By shifting the narrative from one of deprivation to one of discovering nutritious and enjoyable alternatives, it's possible to foster an environment that encourages rather than restricts dietary improvement.

Involving children in the kitchen is a powerful way to encourage healthier eating habits from a young age. Making meal planning and preparation a shared activity not only educates them about nutrition but also equips them with valuable cooking skills. This hands-on approach can pique their interest in whole foods over ultra-processed alternatives. As you explore new recipes and ingredients together, mealtime becomes an adventure in wellness, laying the foundation for lifelong healthy eating habits. It's a chance to instill an appreciation for nutritious foods, transforming the dietary changes you're striving for into a fun, family-oriented journey towards better health.

Creating a supportive environment for dietary changes extends beyond the home and into the workplace. While cooking with co-workers isn't practical, fostering a culture of health within the office is achievable and beneficial. Encouraging the office to engage in healthy choices can start with simple initiatives like bringing in nutritious snacks for break times or organizing healthy potlucks. If you're in a leadership position, you can influence the availability of healthier food options during meetings or in the company pantry. Proposing wellness challenges or sharing educational resources about nutritious eating can also inspire colleagues to make healthier choices. These efforts can contribute to a workplace atmosphere that values and supports the well-being of all its members, creating a ripple effect of positive change across the organization.

Furthermore, as the boss or leader in the office, championing a culture of health can have transformative effects. Introducing healthy and tasty options for office lunches or snack breaks can inspire a shift towards better eating habits among your peers. Surprisingly, people often welcome such initiatives more warmly than anticipated, appreciating the effort towards improving collective well-being.

Expanding the circle of support to include the workplace

not only enhances individual health journeys but also fosters a community spirit focused on well-being. Setting shared goals, celebrating achievements, and navigating challenges together can make the process enriching and fulfilling. Let mealtimes become a cornerstone for building stronger connections and nourishing both body and soul, within the family and amongst colleagues.

We must consider that the path to healthier eating is both a personal and collective journey which can involve our greater family, friends and co-workers. Some of these people may object to changes you make to your diet and lifestyle. Others may want to be on board from the very beginning. By weaving compassion, understanding, and inclusivity into the fabric of this journey, we can overcome obstacles, build supportive networks, and embrace a lifestyle that cherishes nutritional richness and communal well-being.

What's For Lunch?

When considering the ideal lunch, especially in anticipation of a demanding afternoon and avoiding a slump, the composition of this midday meal takes on paramount importance. Imagine you are the client in this scenario. If you're placing your trust in a lawyer with a crucial 2 pm hearing on your behalf, what would you like them to eat for lunch? You'd instinctively prefer they opt for a meal that fuels their mental acuity and physical stamina. This scenario extends beyond specific professions, highlighting a universal need for meals that support rather than detract from our performance in any task requiring precision and focus.

The cornerstone of such a meal includes fresh vegetables, complex carbohydrates, and lean proteins. Fresh fruit is an ideal snack. These components offer a balanced release of energy, essential nutrients, and satiety, which are all crucial for maintaining concentration and productivity through the latter part of the day. Unlike the temporary allure of fast food or the simplicity of bread-heavy options prevalent in fast-casual dining, these whole foods provide the body with what it truly needs to function at its peak.

Fast food or "fast casual" establishments that tout themselves as healthier alternatives still pose significant challenges for those seeking nutritious meals with minimal ultra-processed foods (UPFs). While these venues may offer the allure of convenience and a façade of healthiness, many of their menu options are high in calories yet low in nutritional value, relying heavily on pre-made, frozen or reheated items laden with refined carbohydrates.

The reality is that these meals can lead to rapid spikes in blood sugar, followed by sharp declines, which are detrimental to maintaining energy and focus, particularly for professionals like attorneys who depend on steady cognitive function for peak performance. Furthermore, although some fast casual restaurants provide options that seem wholesome, truly healthy choices often require customizing orders such as substituting dressings, adding extra protein, or omitting certain UPF ingredients, to avoid hidden sugars and unhealthy seed oils. This necessity for vigilance highlights the difficulty in navigating menus at establishments that market health but deliver meals that may undermine long-term well-being and professional productivity.

The most effective strategy for ensuring you consume a nutritious lunch is to take control of its preparation. Making your lunch or engaging in meal prep allows for the selection of high-quality ingredients and the ability to tailor meals to your dietary needs and preferences. This approach not only guarantees a meal that is conducive to sustained mental and physical performance but also aligns with a holistic perspective on health and wellness.

Incorporating a variety of colorful vegetables ensures a broad spectrum of vitamins and antioxidants, fresh fruit provides natural sugars for a quick energy boost, and complex carbohydrates, like those from whole grains or sweet potatoes, offer long-lasting energy. Lean protein sources, whether from animal or plant-based options, support muscle maintenance and satiety. Together, these elements compose a meal that genuinely enhances a professional's ability to perform in the afternoon, ensuring they are as sharp and focused at the end of the day as they were at the start.

So, what do we eat for lunch? In an era rich with information, the internet, apps, and a multitude of books offer endless guidance on creating the ideal, nutritious lunch. The availability of countless meal plans and dietary advice means we're never short on healthy eating inspiration. There are countless pre-made meal plans that do have healthy options if you so choose. Thus, I'll bypass an exhaustive exploration of lunch concepts readily available through these resources. Instead, let's focus on a handful of practical, nourishing lunch ideas specifically curated for the professional navigating a bustling schedule.

It's also pivotal to mention the evolution of lunchboxes, which have transcended their former simplicity. Today's versions offer insulation to maintain meal freshness and appropriate temperatures, as well as compartments for ingredient separation. This innovation simplifies the process of enjoying a range of wholesome meals, irrespective of your location during the day.

Let's also address a common barrier: the assertion of not having enough time. Morning routines might be hectic, especially for those juggling responsibilities like getting kids ready for school. However, labeling this as a reason to skip preparing a healthy lunch is, more often than not, an excuse. The truth is, with a bit of planning and prioritization, integrating meal prep into your routine is entirely feasible. Many find success in allocating a specific time during the week for preparing lunches in advance. This not only streamlines your mornings but also ensures you have nutritious meals at the ready, helping you avoid the temptation of less healthy, convenient options.

Embracing lunch as a pivotal meal in your day is about more than just filling up; it's an opportunity to genuinely enjoy foods that nourish and satisfy you. Skimping on lunch or packing items you're indifferent about isn't just counterproductive, it undermines your day's nutritional foundation and you may even ditch what you brought for the burger around the corner.

Unlike dinner, which may cater to the preferences of a family or group, lunch offers a unique, personal space to indulge in your favorite healthy foods. This meal is your chance to focus solely on what you crave and enjoy. Dive into high-quality, healthy ingredients that make your midday meal something to look forward to. It's not merely about sustenance but about pleasure and satisfaction from foods that fuel your body and spirit for the afternoon ahead.

Navigating office culture while transitioning to healthier lunch habits can sometimes feel like a tightrope walk. Choosing to opt out of the communal takeout order or unveiling a lunch box filled with nutritious alternatives might draw comments or even teasing from colleagues. It's essential, however, not to let this deter you. Remember, your dietary choices are a personal part of your journey toward better health and productivity, not a subject for consensus.

Leading by example is a powerful method of influence, regardless of your position within the office hierarchy. By consistently choosing healthier food options and demonstrating the positive impact on your energy and focus, you can become a catalyst for change in your workplace. When colleagues notice the tangible benefits of your dietary choices, what starts as curiosity can evolve into inspiration.

Furthermore, introducing healthier food options for team lunches or breaks plays a crucial role in fostering an office culture that values well-being. Sharing a platter of fresh fruits and vegetables during meetings, or choosing catered meals from outlets that prioritize nutritious offerings, not only diversifies the palate but also sets a precedent for mindful eating. These actions serve as subtle nudges, encouraging others to consider their own food choices without the need for overt persuasion.

It's also beneficial to engage in open discussions about the reasons behind your food choices when appropriate, of course. Educating peers about the benefits of whole foods over processed alternatives can demystify healthy eating, making it more approachable and desirable. This doesn't mean preaching or judging others' choices but rather sharing insights and experiences that highlight the positive aspects of nutritious eating.

In essence, embracing healthier lunches and promoting a culture of wellness in the workplace is an opportunity to lead by example, inspire change, and contribute to a collective shift towards healthier living. Your commitment to nutritious eating, despite potential comments or jests, not only benefits your own health but can also influence your office environment in a profoundly positive way. Let your lunchbox be a testament to your dedication to wellness, and in time, you may just find others following your lead.

Chapter 6: The Impact Of Hydration On Vitality And Vigor

Hydration is not just about quenching thirst; it's a cornerstone of our physical and mental health. Every cell, tissue, and organ in our body needs water to function properly. For busy professionals, including attorneys and other high-pressure fields, maintaining optimal hydration is essential for peak performance. Despite this, many often neglect their water intake, either due to hectic schedules or the prevalence of dehydrating beverages like coffee and alcohol.

Alcohol, in particular, poses a significant challenge to hydration. Its diuretic effect leads to increased fluid loss, contributing to dehydration. This is especially concerning considering the reliance on alcohol that some professionals might develop as a coping mechanism for stress. However, the irony is that the dehydration caused by alcohol (and caffeinated drinks) can adversely affect the very capabilities they rely on. Dehydration can lead to diminished cognitive functions, affecting concentration, decision-making, and overall mental acuity. This is crucial for professionals whose effectiveness depends on their mental sharpness. Dehydration, even in mild forms, can impair attention, executive function, and motor coordination. This implies that regular hydration isn't just a health issue, but a professional necessity.

Understanding and addressing proper hydration is not just about physical well-being, but about maintaining the high level of cognitive function required for success. This insight forms a compelling argument for reevaluating one's hydration habits, particularly in terms of reducing alcohol and caffeine intake, which are commonly used yet counterproductive in terms of maintaining optimal hydration levels.

As we delve deeper into the importance of hydration, especially for professionals whose cognitive functions are integral to their success, it's essential to underscore the need for plain, filtered water in our daily regimen. While the market is inundated with a variety of beverages like sodas, artificially sweetened drinks, and seltzers, none can replace the fundamental benefits that plain water offers.

Water is the most natural and effective hydrator available to us. Its role in our body is irreplaceable. It aids in digestion, regulates body temperature, and facilitates numerous bodily functions. For those of us who are accustomed to starting their day with coffee, a diuretic, the importance of incorporating plain water into their morning routine cannot be overstated. Drinking water first thing in the morning helps rehydrate the body after a night's sleep, kick-starts metabolism, and prepares the body and brain for the day ahead.

Making a conscious effort to drink plain, filtered water is crucial. Other beverages, while enjoyable, often contain sugars, artificial sweeteners, and other additives that do not provide the same hydration benefits as water. They can also contribute to a false sense of hydration, masking the body's actual need for water. Later in this chapter we will offer a delicious and hydrating alternative to plain water if you are looking for additional options to drink throughout the day (spoiler alert: it's unsweetened tea.)

The importance of electrolytes in hydration is another aspect that warrants attention. Electrolytes, such as sodium, potassium, and magnesium, are vital for maintaining the body's proper fluid balance and are lost through sweat. For those of us with a strenuous routine or those who exercise regularly, replenishing these electrolytes is important to maintain optimal hydration levels. While there are various electrolyte-infused drinks available, these often come with added sugars and calories. A healthier approach is to consume electrolytes through a balanced diet or unsweetened electrolyte-enhanced water, without unnecessary additives.

For professionals aiming to maintain peak cognitive and physical performance, prioritizing the intake of plain, filtered water is a simple yet effective step. It's about retraining our habits and preferences, recognizing the intrinsic value of water in our daily routine. By doing so, we not only ensure proper hydration but also support our overall health, paving the way for enhanced professional efficacy and personal well-being.

The Subtle Yet Insidious Grip Of Alcohol

In the world of law, where precision and clarity are paramount, there's an often-overlooked factor that can significantly impact both: our relationship with alcohol. As the author, I approach this topic not from a place of judgment, but from a personal understanding and a deep sense of compassion. Having navigated my own challenges with alcohol over the years, I recognize the subtleties and nuances of its role in our lives, particularly in high-pressure professions. This isn't a lecture; it's an open conversation about reevaluating our habits for a clearer, more focused life.

As we embark on this candid discussion about alcohol, I want to begin with a personal reflection. My journey with alcohol, like many others, has had its ups and downs. I've experienced firsthand how easy it is to let a casual drink become a regular habit, especially in a culture that often glorifies long hours and high stress with the promise of a relaxing drink at the end of the day. Sharing this isn't about casting judgment but about opening a door to understanding and empathy. We're all navigating this complex world, and for many of us, alcohol has played a significant role.

In the legal profession, where the stakes are high and the hours are long, alcohol can often seem like a trusted companion. It's there at networking events, team dinners, and at the end of a grueling day in court. The narrative around it is persuasive: a glass of wine to unwind, a drink to celebrate a successful case, or just a casual beer with colleagues. It's so ingrained in our professional and social fabric that questioning it almost feels like a breach of an unspoken code.

However, it's crucial to recognize the rationalizations we often use to mask overconsumption. "I've had a hard day; I deserve this," or "It's just one drink to help me relax," are phrases many of us have thought or said. While there's nothing inherently wrong with enjoying a drink, the problem arises when it becomes a routine, a coping mechanism, or a way to avoid dealing with stress, anxiety, or other underlying issues. For professionals who pride themselves on their control and ability to manage complex situations, acknowledging this can be challenging. It requires honesty and self-reflection.

In sharing my experiences and observations, my hope is to shed light on the often subtle ways alcohol can become intertwined with our daily lives and professional identities. It's about starting a conversation, one that's free from judgment and filled with compassion and understanding. We all have different paths, and for some, alcohol may never be an issue. For others, it might be a growing concern. Wherever you are on this spectrum, know that your experiences are valid, and taking a moment to reflect on your relationship with alcohol is a courageous and worthwhile endeavor.

The relationship with alcohol can often begin and continue under the guise of social acceptance and perceived control. Moderate drinking, a term that's become subjective in our social fabric, is often seen as a harmless way to unwind or connect with peers. However, even these socially accepted levels of consumption can have a more profound impact than many realize, subtly clouding judgment, reducing clarity, and affecting decision-making.

As legal professionals, clarity of thought and sharp judgment are not just assets but necessities. Every case, client, and decision demands your utmost mental acuity. Alcohol, even in moderate amounts, can subtly erode this clarity. It might start as a slight haze the morning after or a gradual decrease in energy and focus. Over time, this can lead to a decrease in the very skills and abilities that define your professionalism and success. It's a slow shift, often going unnoticed until the effects are too apparent to ignore.

Moreover, the alcohol industry has been incredibly effective in weaving narratives that not only normalize but glorify regular consumption. One of the most pervasive myths is the supposed health benefits of routine alcohol consumption, particularly regarding red wine. Claims of antioxidants and heart health benefits are often touted, overshadowing the broader health implications. While certain studies suggest moderate wine consumption might have some health benefits, these are frequently overstated and do not consider the comprehensive health risks associated with alcohol. The truth is, any potential benefits of antioxidants in wine can be obtained more safely and effectively through a diet rich in fruits and vegetables, without the adverse effects of alcohol.

It's essential to critically evaluate the messages we receive from the alcohol industry and to understand the real impact of alcohol on our mental clarity, health, and professional performance. This isn't about fear-mongering or promoting abstinence for everyone; it's about empowering informed choices and understanding that even moderate, socially-accepted drinking isn't as benign as it's often portrayed. As professionals committed to excellence in every aspect of our lives, reevaluating the role of alcohol and its subtle yet insidious grip on us is not just beneficial; it's necessary for maintaining the standards we set for ourselves and our careers.

Redefining Passion For Wine And Spirits

The appreciation of fine wine and spirits, such as whiskey, is often celebrated as a mark of sophistication and good taste, particularly in circles where success and achievement are highly valued. From my experience with high achievers, it's clear that collecting rare bottles, discussing vintages, and gifting high-end spirits can indeed be part of a genuine passion for the craftsmanship and history behind these beverages. However, what I've observed is that for some, this interest can serve as a mask for addictive behaviors and excessive drinking habits. Recognizing this fine line between genuine passion and potential dependency is crucial.

For professionals accustomed to long hours and intense pressures, it's easy for the line between connoisseurship and excessive consumption to blur. A glass of fine whiskey to unwind after a successful endeavor or a bottle of exquisite wine at dinner can quickly become a daily necessity rather than an occasional indulgence. The culture of collecting and appreciating can inadvertently provide a socially acceptable cover for dependency.

Genuine appreciation for wine and spirits involves more than mere consumption. It's about understanding the history, the meticulous craft of production, and the unique characteristics that define each bottle. It's savoring each sip and respecting the drink for its qualities, not solely for its intoxicating effects. Conversely, using these interests as a justification for excessive drinking often involves prioritizing alcohol content over the experience, increasing frequency of consumption, or relying on alcohol to relax or feel normal.

Regularly assessing your drinking habits and motivations is essential. Are you reaching for that bottle of whiskey out of genuine interest in tasting and savoring it, or is it becoming a crutch after a stressful day? Does your social life or leisure time primarily revolve around alcohol? Reflecting on questions like these can offer valuable insights into your relationship with alcohol.

Consider how alcohol impacts your personal and professional life. Are you as sharp, focused, and effective as you could be, or does alcohol subtly diminish your performance? How does drinking affect your relationships, health, and overall well-being? Being honest about these impacts is crucial for understanding whether your appreciation for alcohol has crossed into excessive territory.

While genuine passion for wine and spirits can enrich life, it's vital to remain vigilant about their role in your life. Regular self-assessment, understanding your motivations for drinking, and honestly evaluating alcohol's impact on your personal and professional life are crucial steps in ensuring that your appreciation remains healthy and does not become a cover for dependency. As a legal professional, maintaining a balanced and honest relationship with alcohol is integral to your success and well-being.

The illusion of control is a familiar concept. Lawyers, skilled in navigating complex legal systems and negotiations, often develop a heightened sense of control over their work and lives. However, this perceived mastery can create a false sense of security, especially in personal habits like drinking. Professionals in demanding fields may believe they have their alcohol consumption under control, viewing it as a deserved reward or necessary relaxation tool. Yet, this perceived control can be misleading and potentially harmful.

The belief that one can manage their drinking without adverse effects often stems from the broader cultural acceptance of alcohol, particularly in professional settings. Social events, networking, and even casual meetings often involve drinking, making alcohol a staple for socialization and relaxation. This routine integration of alcohol into various aspects of life can foster a false belief in complete control over consumption. However, the line between control and compulsion can be finer than perceived, with transitions often gradual and imperceptible.

Understanding and acknowledging the potential for alcohol to transcend casual indulgence is crucial. It requires honest self-assessment and, at times, willingness to seek help and make changes. True control is not just about managing external aspects of life; it involves managing well-being and recognizing when habits no longer serve you. By maintaining vigilance and mindfulness of your relationship with alcohol, you safeguard against compromising health, happiness, or professional integrity.

For those opting to reduce or eliminate alcohol, the journey often reveals unexpected benefits. Many report newfound clarity, seeing life more vividly and making decisions more deliberately. This clarity can enhance professional focus and performance. Additionally, energy levels often increase, as alcohol's depressant effects diminish. Better sleep quality, improved physical health, and enhanced overall resilience are common outcomes, fostering a deeper understanding of personal needs and values.

Navigating reduced alcohol consumption is a nuanced journey, especially in high-stress environments where alcohol serves both as a social lubricant and coping mechanism. The key lies in mindful choices aligned with a desire for a balanced life. Establish clear, realistic goals, understand triggers prompting drinking, and consider gradual reduction rather than abrupt cessation. Seek support from peers, counselors, or support groups. Embrace alternative activities and new sources of satisfaction. Each step forward, no matter how small, contributes positively to a healthier, more fulfilling life.

The legal community acknowledges the unique pressures faced by its members, offering confidential assistance programs tailored to professionals struggling with substance use. These programs provide counseling, peer support, and intervention services, recognizing the demands of legal work and promoting health and well-being.

Fostering a culture of support within the workplace and broader legal community is essential. Open dialogue about stress and well-being, destigmatizing alcohol struggles, and encouraging help-seeking behaviors shift from silent endurance to collective support and health

Committing to mindful consumption entails awareness of drinking motivations and impacts. It's understanding the line between moderate use and dependency and recognizing when alcohol ceases to serve. By embracing honest self-reflection and making informed choices, you cultivate a healthier, balanced relationship with alcohol, preserving judgment, health, and professional success.

Discovering The World Of Teas

As we shift away from dehydrating alcohol, you should get excited about incorporating new, healthy and hydrating beverages into your daily routines. As noted previously, the beverage market is flooded with drinks that are deceptively harmful, packed with sugars and additives that do our bodies no favors. Regular sodas, energy drinks, and even fruit juices, often perceived as healthier options, are essentially liquid sugar, stripping away the beneficial fibers found in whole fruits and leaving behind a high concentration of natural sugars. Consider this: would you typically consume an apple, a banana, and an orange in one sitting? Probably not. Yet, many don't think twice about drinking the equivalent in fruit juice or soda, inadvertently ingesting a significant amount of sugar.

Diet sodas, while free from sugar, are not without their faults, containing artificial sweeteners and other chemicals that can disrupt our metabolic processes. Educated people disagree on whether artificial sweeteners, in low amounts, are harmful or may still spike insulin responses. We can likely all agree that reducing or eliminating diet soda is likely more beneficial than not. Even seltzer, though a better option and one of my personal favorites, has its downsides, such as higher acidity levels from the carbonation. While there's likely nothing inherently wrong with enjoying seltzer water or a diet soda, those aiming to elevate their hydration practices might look for even healthier alternatives.

If you are looking for a healthy alternative to plain water, we find ourselves exploring the delightful and diverse world of teas. As we pivot towards these infused wonders, we enter a realm where hydration meets flavor, tradition, and a myriad of health benefits. Tea, in its infinite variety, offers a bridge between the necessity of hydration and the pleasure of taste, making it an exemplary companion to water in our daily lives.

Delving into the diverse world of teas, we uncover not just a treasure trove of flavors but also a rich tradition of health benefits, each variety offering unique advantages. Green tea, in particular, stands out for its extensive health benefits, attributed primarily to its rich content of catechins. These potent antioxidants, including (-)-epicatechin (EC), (-)-epicatechin-3-gallate (ECG), (-)-epigallocatechin (EGC), and especially (-)-epigallocatechin-3-gallate (EGCG), offer protective properties against oxidative stress and chronic diseases. A recent review highlighted the anticarcinogenic, anti-inflammatory, and cardiovascular benefits of green tea catechins, underscoring the beverage's significant health-promoting potential (Reygaert, 2017).

Herbal teas, from the calming chamomile to digestion-aiding peppermint, each bring their wellness benefits to the table, offering natural remedies for various ailments. Beyond their therapeutic effects, certain teas, notably green tea, have been associated with weight management benefits. The compounds found in green tea not only contribute to fat oxidation but also enhance metabolic rate, presenting a natural adjunct to diet and exercise for those managing their weight.

Regular consumption of tea, with its array of antioxidants and healthful compounds, supports cardiovascular health and can contribute to a reduced risk of type 2 diabetes. Moreover, the ritualistic nature of tea drinking offers mental and emotional benefits, aiding in stress reduction and promoting a sense of well-being.

The importance of choosing beverages that support rather than compromise our health by prioritizing clean, filtered water, we lay the foundation for optimal hydration, essential for every cellular function in our body. Cutting back on or eliminating alcohol and sugary drinks, we sidestep a host of potential health issues, from disrupted sleep patterns to heightened risk of chronic diseases. And by replacing these with healthful alternatives like tea, we not only hydrate but also imbibe a myriad of compounds beneficial for our health.

Tea, with its vast spectrum of flavors and health benefits, exemplifies the perfect harmony between enjoyment and wellness. It stands as a testament to the power of mindful hydration, a practice that not only quenches thirst but also supports our overall health and vitality. As we move forward, let us carry the insights from this chapter into our daily routines, making hydration a central pillar of a vibrant, energetic life.

In embracing these principles, we do more than just drink; we engage in a practice of self-care that supports our highest levels of performance and well-being. The impact of hydration on vitality and vigor is undeniable, and with each conscious choice we make, we step closer to a life of enhanced health and sustained energy. Let this be a call to action; a reminder that in the simple act of choosing what we drink, we hold the power to significantly influence our health and quality of life.

Chapter 7: Pathways To Joy And Emotional Resilience

Physical health and emotional health are intricately intertwined, each influencing and supporting the other in profound ways. Embracing hobbies and engaging in recreational activities are not just enjoyable pastimes; they are vital components of a holistic approach to maintaining overall health. Rediscovering the simple yet profound joys that once filled our childhood can significantly reduce stress and enhance emotional well-being. A phrase I like to think about is "Everything I like to do are things I did when I was 12," which underscores the purity and unadulterated happiness found in activities from a simpler time, often before the complexities of adult life and the digital age.

Returning to such joys reconnects us with a part of ourselves that was creative, adventurous, and unburdened by the relentless connectivity of today's world. Engaging in these simple pleasures not only nurtures our emotional health but also helps us reclaim a sense of peace and contentment that modern life often obscures.

For professionals, especially in demanding fields, the pull of a career often sidelines these essential activities. However, integrating hobbies into our lives is crucial for emotional resilience. These activities provide an outlet for creativity and relaxation, key to a balanced life necessary for sustaining high performance in professional environments. Engaging in hobbies with family not only enriches personal relationships but also ensures these pursuits do not detract from family time. Instead, they enhance it, demonstrating to our loved ones the importance of maintaining a balanced lifestyle.

In addition to revisiting childhood joys, this chapter discusses the importance of creating dedicated spaces in the home and office that encourage creativity and organization. These personalized spaces not only foster productivity and innovation but also serve as sanctuaries for relaxation and creativity, essential for maintaining mental clarity and emotional health.

Therapy, too, plays a pivotal role in supporting emotional resilience. For legal professionals and others facing high levels of stress, therapy offers not just a means to address and manage challenges but also acts as a proactive tool for enhancing communication, understanding, and overall well-being. Whether through individual sessions, couples counseling, or family therapy, embracing therapeutic support can significantly improve personal and professional relationships, providing crucial tools for navigating life's complexities.

This chapter invites readers to rediscover the joy in creative expression and leisure activities, understand the value of organized and inspiring environments, and recognize the profound benefits of therapeutic engagement. By integrating these elements, legal professionals can forge a path toward a more balanced, fulfilling life that harmonizes professional demands with personal and emotional satisfaction.

Pursuing Hobbies and Expressive Interests

Exploring hobbies and expressive interests is crucial for achieving a balanced and fulfilling life. These activities not only serve as powerful tools for managing stress but also encourage you to either revisit past interests or embark on new ventures.

The range of options is vast and varied, including artistic endeavors like painting, sculpture, and clay work, as well as intellectually stimulating pursuits such as reading, writing, or playing a musical instrument. For those who enjoy tactile engagements, hobbies like sewing, crafting or model airplane building can provide immense satisfaction. Others might find joy in remodeling classic cars, working on DIY projects at home, or gardening.

The benefits of engaging in these creative outlets are manifold. Engaging in a hobby is not just a way to pass time; it's a form of stress relief, a means to improve mental health, and a path to personal fulfillment. These activities provide an escape from the pressures of daily life, offering a space to unwind and engage in something purely for the joy of it. The focus and concentration required for these activities can be a form of meditation, clearing the mind and providing a sense of calm and tranquility.

For individuals balancing the demands of both a career and a family, the challenge of finding time for personal hobbies can seem insurmountable. Yet, it's precisely within this nexus of work and family where hobbies can serve a dual purpose. They become not just a means for personal fulfillment but also a conduit for enriching family relationships. Embracing hobbies in the context of family life transforms them from solitary pursuits into shared ventures that deepen connections and create lasting memories.

Children, with their innate curiosity and eagerness to explore, can be the perfect companions for rediscovering old passions or embarking on new ones. Engaging in hobbies together is not merely about passing time; it's about seizing opportunities for quality interaction that can strengthen the familial bond. These shared experiences can range widely, from the simple joys of nature walks, where the changing seasons offer new wonders at every turn, to the collaborative creativity of arts and crafts projects that turn imaginations into tangible creations.

Moreover, integrating hobbies into family life is a powerful way to model lifelong learning and curiosity for children. It demonstrates the value of dedicating time to activities that bring joy and satisfaction beyond the realms of work and school. Whether it's through cooking meals together, where each dish can be an adventure in flavors and techniques, or embarking on DIY home projects, where the sense of achievement is shared, these experiences can teach invaluable lessons about persistence, creativity, and the joy of accomplishment.

In our connected world, the barriers to entering new realms of hobby and interest are lower than ever before. The internet has democratized access to knowledge, with platforms like online courses, forums, and particularly, the vast repository of tutorials on platforms like YouTube, opening up avenues for learning that were previously constrained by geographical and financial limitations. This digital landscape allows for the exploration of hobbies that once might have felt inaccessible, enabling individuals to delve into areas like digital art, programming, music production, or even languages, all from the comfort of their home.

The drive to explore these hobbies, either for personal fulfillment or as shared family activities, underscores their role far beyond mere leisure. They stand as vital pillars supporting a balanced lifestyle, fostering not just individual growth but also enriching our relationships with loved ones. The pursuit of hobbies provides a meaningful diversion from the day-to-day, infusing our lives with variety and opportunities for discovery. For professionals entrenched in the rigors of careers like law, dedicating time to hobbies and creative endeavors is more than a luxury, it's a crucial component of a sustainable lifestyle that prioritizes wellness and personal satisfaction alongside professional achievement.

Organization Of Space And Unused Corners

The concept of meticulously organizing both home and office cannot be overstated, particularly for those in professions that demand high levels of concentration and creativity. This approach extends beyond the mere aesthetic appeal; it's a fundamental component of fostering an environment conducive to productivity and innovation. Just as we emphasize the transformation of underused corners into creative sanctuaries at home, applying similar principles of organization and dedicated space creation in the workplace is equally important.

A clear workspace not only streamlines the immediate environment but also significantly enhances focus and creativity. The removal of unnecessary clutter allows the mind to operate without distraction, fostering a fertile ground for innovative thoughts and solutions.

In high-stress careers, particularly in this day and age where we likely work both from home and an office, having well-organized spaces is essential. It's not just about decluttering or having a neat desk; it's about creating an environment that mirrors the sanctity of your creative space at home. This could mean designating a specific area in your office where you can step away from your usual work tasks and engage in brief creative pursuits or mindfulness exercises. Just as a corner of your home can be transformed into a zone for hobbies and relaxation, a section of your office can serve as a mini-retreat, equipped with items that help shift your mind away from work-related stress.

The challenge of maintaining such order increases when family or others share the home. However, organization can be a collective effort that benefits everyone. Turning decluttering into a family project not only eases the workload but also helps instill a sense of order and responsibility in all household members. Everyone's participation ensures that each person respects the shared spaces, contributing to a harmonious home environment conducive to everyone's well-being.

Moreover, seeking inspiration and motivation from television shows about decluttering can provide practical tips and the motivation needed to start organizing. Watching transformations as guided by experts can spark the enthusiasm to create similar changes in one's own spaces.

The importance of this organization and space designation extends to virtual environments as well. Digital clutter can be just as distracting and overwhelming as physical disarray. Therefore, organizing your digital workspace, creating clear, dedicated folders for different projects, and maintaining a streamlined email inbox are crucial steps in mirroring the physical organization into your digital realm.

Furthermore, the benefits of creating and organizing these spaces are manifold. They not only enhance focus and efficiency by minimizing distractions but also significantly contribute to stress reduction. Having a go-to creative nook at home or a tranquil corner in the office can serve as a psychological cue, signaling your brain to transition from work mode to a state of relaxation and creativity. This physical and mental separation is vital for sustaining long-term productivity and well-being.

Beyond workspaces, consider carving out a personal sanctuary tailored to your interests and needs: be it a reading nook, a corner for a painting easel, or a dedicated space for your yoga mat and meditation practice. Creating these dedicated areas in your home does more than just allocate physical space for hobbies and relaxation; it symbolizes a commitment to nurturing your personal growth and emotional well-being. In the rush and responsibilities of professional life, having a private nook to unwind, reflect, or engage in pleasurable activities can serve as a critical buffer against stress and burnout.

Moreover, these personal sanctuaries offer a unique opportunity to disconnect from the digital world and reconnect with oneself. They can become the settings where creativity flourishes, where new ideas and perspectives are born, and where the mind finds the peace and quiet needed to rejuvenate.

Ultimately, the organization of our physical and digital spaces is reflective of our commitment to balancing the demands of our professional lives with the need for personal development and leisure. For professionals navigating the complexities of careers in law and other high-stress fields, investing in the creation and organization of these sanctuaries is not just a luxury; it's a necessary component of a holistic approach to living.

Therapy For Burnout And Familial Relationships

Maintaining emotional health is as critical as any legal strategy. Therapy, in its various forms, emerges as an invaluable tool in this quest for emotional balance and well-being. Whether it's individual therapy, couples counseling, or family therapy, the importance of these therapeutic avenues in nurturing and enhancing emotional health cannot be overstated.

For lawyers, the professional hazards can extend beyond mere stress and burnout. Depending on the area of practice, many lawyers face secondary traumatic stress disorder from handling cases involving severe trauma, such as bodily injury, violence or abuse. These experiences can profoundly impact a lawyer's emotional and psychological state. Individual therapy provides a safe space for lawyers to express themselves, process these intense emotions, and learn coping mechanisms to manage the psychological toll of their work. This is crucial not only for the lawyer's personal health but also for maintaining their effectiveness and ethical standards in their professional roles.

Therapy offers more than just a remedy for turmoil; it's a proactive measure for emotional upkeep. For legal professionals navigating an environment riddled with stress and challenge, therapy provides a haven to decompress and strategize. Individual therapy focuses on personal growth and self-awareness, aiding professionals in better managing job pressures, balancing life, and honing decision-making skills. In the realm of relationships, couples therapy becomes crucial, not just in times of strife but as a preventive measure to fortify partnerships against the inevitable pressures of a demanding career.

Family therapy, too, holds a significant place. In a profession where long hours and high demands can strain family dynamics, this form of therapy offers a collective platform for open communication and problem-solving. It ensures that familial relationships remain resilient and supportive, even when professional life becomes overwhelming. Ignoring emerging issues within the family structure, especially under the pressure of a demanding career, can lead to a build-up of unresolved conflicts and emotional distance. Addressing problems early through family therapy prevents them from festering and growing into larger, more complex disputes over time. By fostering a routine of honest dialogue and collective coping strategies, family therapy helps maintain a strong family foundation, crucial for withstanding the vicissitudes of life. This proactive approach not only alleviates immediate stress but also strengthens the family's ability to navigate future challenges together, preserving the family's overall health and unity.

One of the most significant benefits of therapy is the objective perspective it provides. Therapists are skilled in offering unbiased insights and reflective guidance, often shedding light on overlooked aspects of a situation. This external viewpoint is invaluable in both personal and professional contexts, helping to identify underlying issues and craft effective strategies for resolution.

However, within the legal community and many other professional realms, there's often a stigma attached to seeking therapy. This perception needs to shift. Recognizing the need for and seeking therapy is not a sign of weakness but a testament to self-awareness and a commitment to overall well-being. It's about building resilience, not just enduring pressure.

In embracing therapy, legal professionals aren't just

addressing immediate problems; they're laying the groundwork for a more balanced, fulfilling life. It's a step towards acknowledging the complexity of our emotional landscape and taking proactive measures to navigate it effectively. Integrating therapy into the routine of a legal professional is an investment in oneself, ensuring that one can be the best version of themselves, both personally and professionally.

Crafting A Balanced Life Through Creativity

The imperative to actively engage in hobbies and prioritize emotional health cannot be overstated, especially within professions as strenuous and consuming as law. The equilibrium between our professional obligations and personal fulfillment often teeters precariously, making the indulgence in creative outlets not merely a pastime but an essential practice for well-being. These ventures into creativity and hobbies serve as vital escapes, offering us the chance to decompress, to explore facets of ourselves left unattended in the hustle of daily tasks, and to cultivate a richness in life that work alone cannot provide. Far from being mere diversions, they are fundamental to a life that is not only successful but truly satisfying.

The pursuit of emotional health and the exploration of creative avenues do more than enrich our own lives; they set a powerful example for the next generation. Demonstrating to children the importance of balancing hard work with personal passions teaches them invaluable lessons about the multifaceted nature of success and well-being. It underscores the importance of personal growth, the value of mental health care, and the essential role of creativity in a balanced life.

Moreover, embracing the concept of seeking therapy and other forms of emotional support is critical. It's a testament to understanding that achieving optimal performance in our careers and overall quality of life often requires external guidance and reflection. Therapy offers a pathway not just through difficulties but toward personal enlightenment and resilience, enabling us to face both professional challenges and life's complexities with greater clarity and strength.

Engaging in non-work, creative activities provides our work brain with essential breaks, often leading to moments of insight and innovative thinking. Just as Archimedes reportedly discovered the principle of water displacement while taking a bath, our best ideas can emerge when we allow our minds to wander and recharge through creative pursuits. These activities not only refresh our perspectives but also fuel innovation and enhance problem-solving abilities, ultimately contributing to improved decision-making in our professional lives.

As we navigate the demands of our careers, it is crucial to remember what is truly important: the quality of our lives, the depth of our relationships, and the joy we derive from creative expression. Embracing hobbies and creativity not only enriches our personal lives but can also enhance our professional capabilities. Creativity fuels innovation, problem-solving, and can lead to improved logical thinking and decision-making in our work.

Crafting a balanced life through creativity is not just an option but a necessity, especially in demanding professions like law. The Niyama of Tapas, which represents enthusiasm and a fiery passion, is crucial here. It's this burning drive that lawyers often start with but may see wane over time due to professional burnout. Actively engaging in hobbies and prioritizing emotional health reignites this inner fire, maintaining the delicate balance between professional obligations and personal fulfillment.

This isn't merely about passing time; it's about using creativity as an essential tool for well-being, providing the opportunity to decompress, explore unattended facets of our personality, and cultivate a richness in life that work alone cannot achieve. These creative ventures are fundamental to not only achieving success but also ensuring it is deeply satisfying. Engaging in non-work creative activities provides essential breaks for our working brains, often leading to moments of insight and innovative thinking, enhancing problem-solving abilities, and ultimately contributing to improved decision-making in our professional lives.

Final Thoughts: A Continuous Journey Toward Self-Improvement

At the core of our being, there exists an unyielding drive for continuous learning and self-improvement. This journey of becoming the best versions of ourselves transcends the confines of our professional roles, permeating every aspect of our existence, whether as attorneys, parents, partners, or simply as individuals. The aspiration to improve, refine, and excel is a clear reflection of our intrinsic potential for growth and transformation.

Reflecting on the perilous trade-offs of pursuing career success and financial stability at the expense of our long-term health, we recognize the risk involved. The pursuit of immediate professional accomplishments can often precipitate a steep decline in health, leaving many unable to enjoy the fruits of their labor upon reaching the zeniths of their careers or the onset of retirement. It's crucial, then, to reassess such sacrifices, ensuring that our drive for achievement does not undermine our well-being.

Acknowledging and embracing this path toward self-improvement is not merely advantageous; it's crucial for achieving self-fulfillment and actualization, which also happens to be the last of the Eight Limbs of Yoga, Samadhi.

In this light, the concept of Samadhi, or complete enlightenment, represents the ultimate integration of our personal and professional growth. It is a state where heightened awareness and deep peace permeates all aspects of life, offering a profound balance and interconnectedness that extends beyond mere success. Embracing the journey toward Samadhi not only enriches our individual experiences but also enhances our contributions to the legal profession and broader society, setting a benchmark for excellence and holistic health. This enlightened state underscores that true success encompasses not just professional achievements, but also the mastery of inner well-being and harmony.

As Attorney Wellness Advocates, we understand that healthy holistic practices in our daily lives are not peripheral to our success but integral, forming the foundation upon which our capacity to lead, influence, and inspire rests. We recognize the intertwining of wellness and excellence in the legal profession. The principles of health, mindfulness, and continuous learning are not just strategies for personal fulfillment but blueprints for professional mastery. The true measure of success lies not solely in the accolades we accrue but in our commitment to growth, our resilience in the face of adversity, and our dedication to becoming the most authentic, effective versions of ourselves.

As we cultivate compassion and self-care, we have the profound opportunity to elevate the entire legal profession. We have all likely witnessed colleagues grappling with depression, disease, chronic stress, addiction, burnout, and mental health challenges. By extending our learnings and support to others, we contribute to a culture of kindness and ethical excellence. Through our actions, we can inspire and empower fellow attorneys to prioritize their well-being, fostering a community where professional success is not synonymous with personal sacrifice, but thrives on a foundation of holistic health and resilience.

Consider this not the end, but a beginning. A starting point for a deeper exploration into the dimensions of your well-being and a challenge to integrate these principles into your daily practice. Recall the strategy we outlined: confront health challenges as you would crucial evidence in a legal case, facing them directly. Should you find yourself feeling stuck, mentally ensnared by the complexities of life, remember that embarking on a journey of physical self-improvement often paves the way for greater insight into oneself.

This intertwined progression underscores that we are never truly stuck; we are always on the cusp of evolution, poised for growth and ripe for transformation. The pursuit of becoming the best attorney, the most understanding partner, the most nurturing parent, or simply the best version of yourself is a journey worth embarking on. It's a continuous path of learning, growing, and striving for excellence in all we do, acknowledging that the enhancement of our physical well-being can significantly catalyze our mental and emotional resurgence.

Now, I challenge you to take the first step. Begin today, not tomorrow. Integrate what you've learned into your routine, share these practices with others, and commit to the ongoing process of self-improvement. This is your moment to lead by example, to inspire change not just in your own life, but in the lives of those around you. Every small step you take brings you closer to a life of balance, health, and true success. The time to act is now. Embrace this journey with courage and determination, and watch as you transform not only your own life but the very culture of the legal profession.

Convenient Yoga Supplement For Lawyers

As a lawyer, wellness advocate, and yoga instructor well-versed in the pressures of professional life, I present a Convenient Yoga Supplement for Lawyers. This series includes tailored yoga sequences named Destress, Energize, and Relax, each designed to seamlessly fit into the busy schedules of professionals. These sequences are practical, accessible, and serve as a gentle reminder of how refreshing and beneficial a good stretch can be.

Whether you're new to yoga or rediscovering the joys of stretching after a period of inactivity, you'll appreciate how deeply satisfying it can be to reconnect with your body in this way. Engage in these practices to integrate meaningful breaks into your day without needing special preparations.

These practices are rooted in the Hatha tradition. Hatha yoga, a branch of yoga, emphasizes physical exercises to master the body along with mind exercises to withdraw it from external objects. The word "Hatha" can be translated as "force," denoting the system's potent approach to self-transformation through physical disciplines. Hatha yoga practices are designed to align and calm your body, mind, and spirit in preparation for meditation.

Hatha yoga stands out due to its focus on asanas (postures) and pranayama (breathing exercises), which are performed more slowly and with more static posture holds than in some other forms of yoga. This approach not only cultivates physical strength, flexibility, and stamina but also promotes mental clarity and calmness. The practices within the Hatha tradition serve as a gateway to balancing the flow of pranic energy within the body, helping to release blockages and enhance mental and physical equilibrium.

The gentle yet profound practices of Hatha yoga not only make it suitable for practitioners of all levels, including beginners, but also offer immediate relief and long-term benefits. Whether you're dealing with a stiff or sore back, painful feet, wrist pain from extensive typing, or tight hips from prolonged sitting, practicing yoga can feel like receiving a massage from within, one that reaches deeper than any superficial muscle treatment. If you deepen your practice and take classes from an experienced teacher at a yoga studio, there's no telling how great you will feel.

These sequences are designed to be both adaptable and accessible. This approach, reflecting the broader yoga tradition's emphasis on inclusivity and individual adjustment, ensures that the practices can enrich and accommodate a wide audience, offering a path to balance and wellness tailored to the unique demands of daily professional life. This method underscores the importance of balance and adaptability, echoing the demands of a hectic professional life and offering a pathway to physical and mental well-being through yoga.

Recognizing a common concern among professionals, especially lawyers, about yoga being inconvenient, these sequences have been specifically developed to address and overcome that obstacle. The Destress and Energize sequences can be easily performed in the office, possibly with the door closed for privacy, and do not require changing out of work clothes. This flexibility allows for a moment of rejuvenation without stepping away from your professional environment. The Relax sequence, while also adaptable to the workplace, might be more comfortably practiced at the end of the day or at home, as it's conducive to using a mat and possibly changing into more comfortable attire.

Safety And Disclaimer

It is essential to approach these practices with mindfulness and respect for your body's limitations. None of these poses should cause pain; they are intended to offer a beneficial stretch and a moment of mental clarity. If discomfort or pain arises, it's crucial to back off and reassess. Remember that the images provided are just guides; every body will look different based on body type and shape, level of flexibility, and other personal factors. Do not worry if you do not look exactly like these pictures. In fact, I encourage you to read the descriptions of the poses carefully and use the language to primarily guide you, feeling the pose in your body.

Proper form is key to a safe and effective practice, so if you're uncertain about a pose or new to yoga, seeking guidance from a qualified instructor in person is recommended. These poses should feel like rejuvenating stretches for the entire body. Remember, the goal is to support your well-being, not to push through discomfort. If you have physical limitations, chronic health conditions, pregnancy or similar situations, please seek in-person guidance from a qualified instructor, prenatal instructor or physical therapist.

These yoga sequences are more than a physical regimen; they represent a holistic approach to managing stress, enhancing focus, reinvigorating fascial and lymphatic tissue, and cultivating well-being amidst the demands of a legal career. By making yoga a seamless part of your day, you're not only contributing to your physical health but also investing in your mental and emotional resilience.

Destress

Neck Movements: *Greeva Sanchalana*

Sit comfortably with a tall spine. Gently stretch your neck to each side, using your hand for gentle pressure if desired while reaching out with the other hand.

Slowly roll your head in a half-moon shape towards the front only. Avoid rolling towards the back to prevent strain on the neck vertebrae, especially as we age.

Only place light pressure on the hand with your head.

You can also adjust your hand slightly to the back of your neck, angling it downward as you roll forward to the other side.

As stated above, avoid rolling your neck to the back - only side to side and forward.

Sitting Cat-Cow: *Durga Go*

Sit comfortably in your chair with your feet flat on the floor and a tall spine. Place your hands on your knees or the desk in front of you for support and leverage.

Inhale as you arch your back, lifting your head and chest towards the ceiling (Cow), and exhale as you round your spine, tucking your chin towards your chest (Cat). Repeat this movement, syncing your breath with each motion.

Don't overextend the neck to the back or turn from side to side while your head is tipped back.

The movements of sitting Cat Cow are subtle in these images. Remember that while in Cat (this page), you want to exhale your breath and round your back. Inhale in Cow (prior page) while gently looking up and arching your back. Do not overextend your neck to the back, or roll your neck to the back.

Sitting Forward Fold: *Paschimottanasana*

Begin by taking a deep breath and elongating your spine, sitting as tall as possible in your chair. On the exhale, gently lean forward, allowing your head to hang towards the floor. Relax your spine and neck, releasing any tension.

You can place your hands on the floor or gently at the back of your neck for support and comfort. Keep your legs either closed or open, depending on your preference for a deeper stretch. When coming out of the pose, rise slowly to avoid dizziness.

Try to relax your head and let it hang while in a modified forward fold. If you'd like, gently nod your head and turn left and right while it hangs heavy.

Side Lateral Stretch: *Parighasana*

Begin seated in a modification of Gate Pose. Inhale deeply and reach both arms overhead. As you exhale, stretch one arm sideways overhead, maintaining length in the side body of the contracting side.

Avoid collapsing the side body. If comfortable, gently turn your head towards the elongated arm to deepen the stretch.

If you are able, gently turn your neck and look up towards your hand. If this is not comfortable for you, then leave that out.

Seated Twist: *Bharadvajasana*

Begin by sitting upright in a chair. Inhale deeply, elongating the spine and raising one arm. As you exhale, gently twist your torso about 45 degrees to one side, using the chair arms for support and leverage. If comfortable, gradually work towards twisting to 90 degrees or slightly beyond.

Maintain an upright spine throughout the twist. Hold the pose for five deep breaths, endeavoring to deepen the twist with each exhale. This helps to alleviate stress in the lower back and keeps the spine supple.

Twist from the waist up, maintaining full contact of your bottom to the chair. Do not let one hip lift up while you are twisting - push it back down.

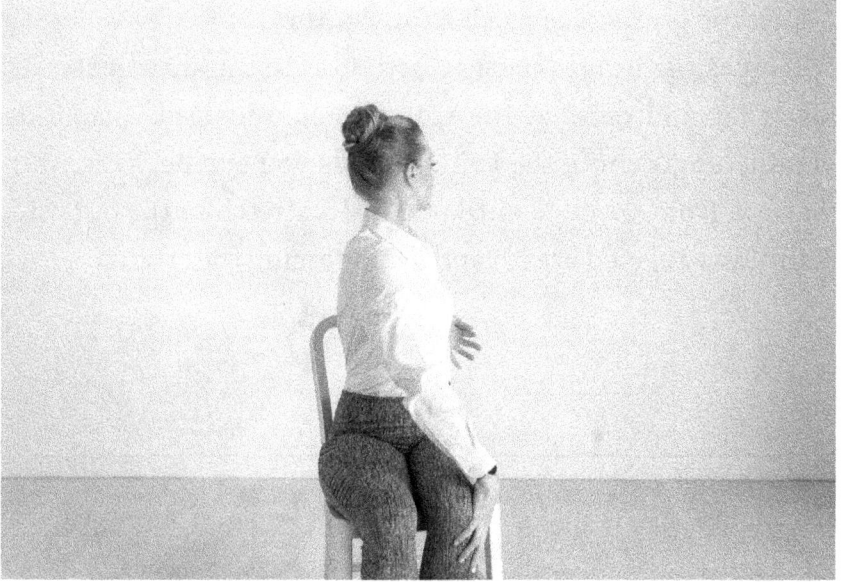

Seated Hip Opener: *Ardha Padmasana*

Begin by sitting comfortably in a chair. Cross one leg over the opposite thigh, allowing the ankle to rest on top of the thigh. Adjust the position as needed for comfort.

If crossing the legs causes discomfort in the knees, extend the lower leg and cross at the shin or ankle instead. Take a deep breath, lengthening the spine, and as you exhale, gently hinge forward from the hips until you feel a stretch in the outer hips. Maintain a relaxed breath and avoid forcing the stretch.

Wrist Stretch: *Bharmanasana*

Begin by sitting or standing in front of a desk. Place your hands on the edge of the desk with palms facing down and fingers pointing towards you, in an outward rotation. Push your hands forward until you feel a gentle stretch in your wrists.

Hold the stretch for a few breaths, maintaining a comfortable level of tension, backing off if necessary.

This pose serves as a counterpose to the repetitive motion of typing and can help alleviate wrist discomfort.

You may not be able to completely rotate your fingers back towards you, as is shown here. That is fine, simply go as far as is comfortable, pushing gently towards your edge of comfort for a relieving stretch.

If your wrists are not used to rotating in this manner, it may require consistent practice to reach a full rotation. The relief you will feel in your wrists and forearms is worth the effort.

Extended Puppy: *Uttana Shishosana*

Stand in front of your desk or the back of a chair, depending on comfort and accessibility. Grasp the edge of the desk or chair with your hands, ensuring your arms are straight and shoulder-width apart. Begin to walk your feet back until your body forms an inverted "V" shape, keeping your legs straight but not locked at the knees.

Allow your head to hang between your arms, and focus on lengthening your spine while maintaining a steady breath. Hold this pose for about a minute, continuing to breathe deeply.

This rejuvenating stretch helps alleviate fatigue and replenishes lost energy.

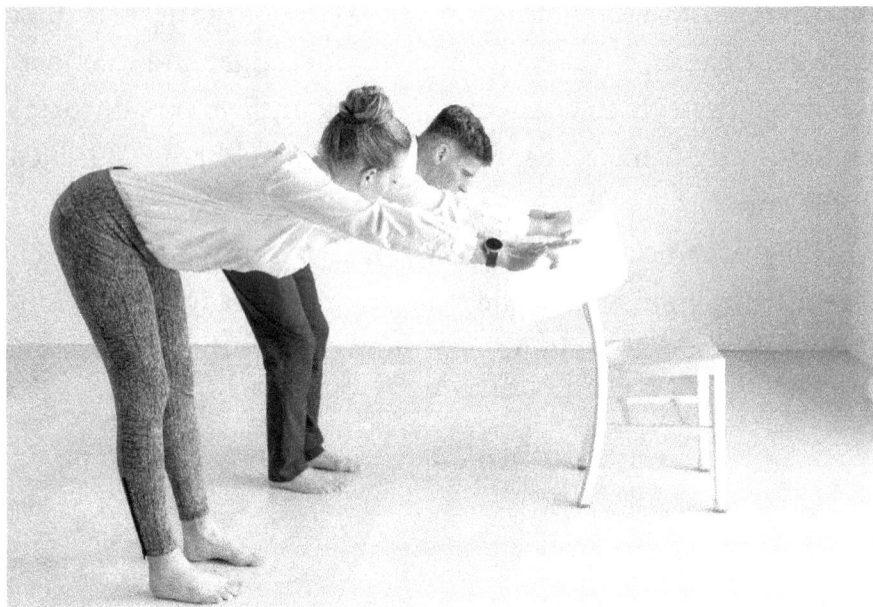

Energize

Standing Crescent Moon: *Urdhva Hastasana*

Begin by standing tall with your feet hip-width apart. Inhale deeply as you reach both arms overhead, lengthening through your spine. On the exhale, gently lean towards the right, creating a crescent shape with your body. Keep your torso facing forward and actively pull your left shoulder back.

If comfortable, turn your head to gaze towards the left and upwards, deepening the stretch along the side of your body. Hold this position for 3-5 deep breaths, feeling the stretch along the left side. Then, repeat on the other side by switching the grip and leaning towards the left. Maintain steady breathing throughout the pose.

Standing Forward Fold: *Uttanasana*

Start in a standing position with your feet hip-width apart. Inhale deeply as you raise your arms overhead, lengthening through the spine. As you exhale, hinge at the hips and fold forward, allowing your arms to hang low towards the ground. You can keep a slight to moderate bend in your knees to ease tension in the hamstrings.

Relax your head and neck, letting them hang heavy. Hold this position for as long as it feels comfortable, focusing on lengthening the spine with each breath.

When coming out of the pose, do so slowly to avoid dizziness, gently rolling up one vertebra at a time.

Keep a microbend in your knees in forward fold.

Don't worry if you cannot reach the floor. Let your arms hang loose or grab opposite elbows.

If forward fold is challenging because you have tight hamstrings, bend your knees as much as you need, resting your stomach on your legs and letting your neck and arms hang loose.

High Lunge Crescent: *Utthita Ashta Chandrasana*

Begin by stepping your right foot forward into a lunge position, ensuring that the knee does not extend beyond the ankle. Extend your back leg straight and engage your core muscles. Inhale deeply as you raise your arms overhead, keeping your shoulders relaxed. Hold the position for 3-5 deep breaths, maintaining stability and balance.

After completing one side, switch to the other leg and repeat the sequence.

For an extra challenge, add a gentle twist by rotating your waist towards the side of the front leg and stretch your arms in line with your legs.

Pyramid Pose: *Parsvottanasana*

Begin by standing with your feet hip-width apart. Step one foot back about 3-4 feet, ensuring that your feet are not in line but slightly wider apart like a regular walking step. Inhale deeply as you raise your arms overhead, lengthening through the spine. As you exhale, hinge at the hips and fold forward over your front leg, keeping your spine long and shoulders square.

Keep your hands either on the floor or on your front leg for support. Hold the pose for several deep breaths, feeling the stretch along the back of the front leg's hamstring. After holding, slowly rise back up to standing.

Your hips should be squared to the front, so you may need to adjust by gently pulling the hip of the back leg forward.

Keep a microbend or a deeper bend in your front leg if you have tight hamstrings.

Standing Twist: *Eka Pada Parivrtta Tadasana*

Begin by standing with your feet hip-width apart and arms by your sides. Inhale deeply as you raise your arms overhead, lifting your knee off the ground. You can grab your knee and pull it closer to the chest, if you choose.

Twist from the waist towards the knee that is elevated. Reach with your arm, rotating towards and past the elevated knee towards the back of the room. Hold the pose for a few breaths. Then, return to center and repeat the twist on the other side. You want to be secure in your balance when you raise your knee before you twist.

Once you are in the twist, you can gently rotate your neck to look at your back hand.

You want to be sure to twist from the waist up, keeping your hips square to the front.

Chair Pose: *Utkatasana*

Begin by standing tall with your feet together or hip-width apart, depending on your preference. Inhale deeply as you raise your arms overhead, palms facing each other. As you exhale, bend your knees and lower your hips as if sitting back into an invisible chair. Keep your chest lifted and core engaged as you reach your arms up towards the ceiling.

Be mindful to keep your knees behind your toes and your thighs parallel to the floor, ensuring proper alignment.. Hold the pose for a few breaths, feeling the grounding energy radiate through your body.

Your knees and feet should be the same distance apart, whether you choose to have your feet and knees close together or hip-distance apart.

Reach up with your arms, if that is comfortable, but do not over-arch your back. Take prayer hands if you find the reaching up to be uncomfortable.

Be mindful of your knees to make sure they are not overextending past your toes. If they are, sit back in your invisible chair more.

Your weight should be mostly pressing back into your heels, not your toes. Try to lift your toes while practicing this position.

Modified Dancer Pose: *Natarajasana*

Begin by standing tall with your feet hip-width apart. Inhale as you raise both arms overhead, lengthening through the spine. On the exhale, bend one knee and flex your foot towards your buttocks. Reach back with the same-side hand and grasp your foot or ankle.

Focus on stretching the quadriceps of the lifted leg while maintaining balance. Simultaneously, reach the opposite arm overhead to enhance the stretch and balance.

You can also lift the leg as much as is comfortable. Maintain a microbend in your standing leg; do not lock out the knee. Some practitioners reach and hold the foot from the inside, this may better keep the shoulder in alignment if you are lifting the leg high.

Breathe while lifting the leg as much as is comfortable without losing form. This balancing pose will improve with practice.

Warrior III: *Virabhadrasana III*

Begin by standing tall with feet hip-width apart. Ensure your shoulders, hips, and ankles are aligned, then press firmly through the soles of your feet. Extend your arms overhead, biceps by your ears. Transfer your weight onto your right leg, lifting your left foot off the floor.

As you hinge forward at the hips, raise your left leg behind you, aiming to bring your chest parallel to the floor and your raised leg in line with your body, forming a "T" shape. Focus on maintaining a strong, straight line from your fingertips to your lifted heel. Repeat on the opposite side.

If reaching forward is too much for you (as shown above), you can place your hands in prayer at the heart center, or "airplane" arms where they are reaching back and down at a 45 degree angle.

Using a chair is a great way to practice reaching forward in Warrior III.

You want to reach for a T-shape in Warrior III, but it is not necessary to lift the leg this high in your practice.

Relax

Child's Pose with Lateral Reach: *Balasana*

Begin on your hands and knees on your mat, spreading your knees wide while keeping the tops of your feet flat against the mat. Lower your belly between your thighs, resting your forehead on the floor or a supportive block to stimulate the vagus nerve for a calming effect.

Extend your arms forward with palms down for a standard pose or alongside your body with palms up for less shoulder engagement.

Enhance this pose by adding a lateral reach: from the standard Child's Pose, crawl your hands to the right to stretch the left side of your body, then to the left to stretch the right side. Remain in the pose as long as comfortable, focusing on steady breathing.

Crawl your hands past each side of the mat, elongating the side body while keeping your head and neck relaxed.

Cat-Cow with Variations: *Durga Go*

Start in a tabletop position, with your wrists directly under your shoulders and your knees under your hips. Inhale as you arch your back, lifting your head and tailbone towards the ceiling for Cow pose. As you exhale, round your spine, tucking your chin towards your chest and drawing your belly button towards your spine for Cat pose.

Inhale the breath while looking up and arching the back in Cow.

Exhale the breath while rounding your spine, dropping your head and tucking in your tailbone in Cat.

For a gentle lateral stretch while doing Cat Cow pose, turn your head and peek over your shoulder to each side while curving your spine in a "C" shape.

For an additional lateral modification while practicing Cat Cow pose, you can reach a leg out to the side, keeping the outstretched foot on the floor facing forward. Press the outer edge of your foot into the floor. If you are able, sit back on your hips as much as is comfortable for a few breaths. Repeat anything you tried on one side, on the other.

Sphinx Pose: *Salamba Bhujangasana*

Lie face down on the mat with your legs extended behind you and the tops of your feet pressing into the floor. Place your forearms on the mat parallel to each other, elbows directly under your shoulders, and palms pressing firmly into the mat. Inhale as you gently lift your chest and upper back off the mat, drawing your shoulder blades down and back to open your chest and lengthen through the crown of your head.

In this pose, your hands should grip the mat to gently pull the chest forward, not push up. Only stretch your neck as much as you are comfortable.

Half Bow Pose: *Ardha Dhanurasana*

Begin by lying on your stomach (prone position) on your yoga mat. From here, bend one knee and reach back with your hand to grasp the foot or ankle of that leg. As you gently pull the foot towards your backside, you will feel a deep stretch in the quadriceps and the front of the thigh.

Maintain steady breathing as you hold the pose for several breaths, focusing on gradually deepening the stretch. If you find it difficult to reach your foot with your hand, you can use a yoga strap looped around your ankle to assist in the stretch.

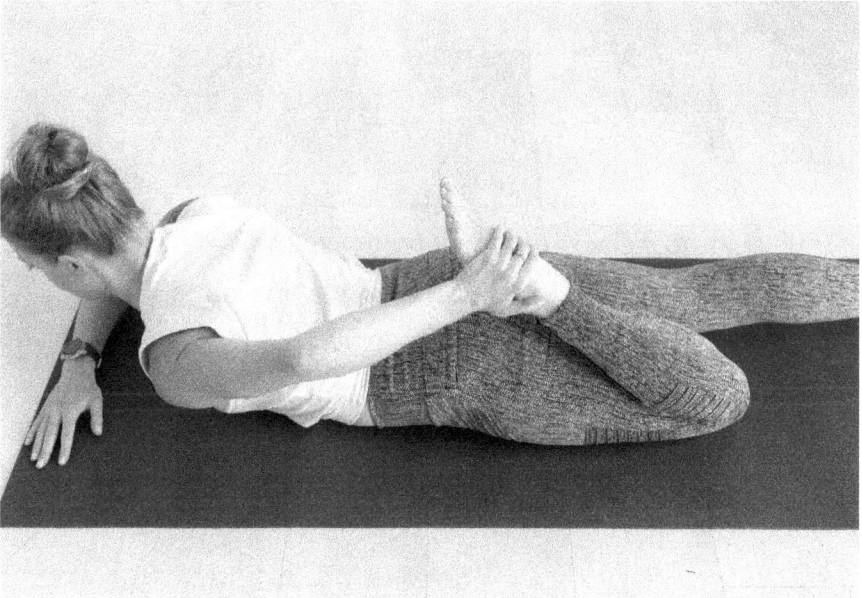

In addition to being a quadricep stretch, Half Bow pose also stretches out the chest, intercostal muscles between the ribs, the pectorals and deltoids.

If you cannot reach your back foot as is shown in this picture, use a yoga strap or a belt to wrap around your ankle.

Reclined Pigeon: *Supta Kapotasana*

Begin by lying on your back with legs extended and arms by your side. Bend your knees to place the soles of your feet on the ground, then create a figure four by crossing your right ankle over your left knee. Flex your right foot and lift the left foot from the floor.

Weave your right arm through the leg opening and bring your left arm around the outside of the left leg to clasp your hands either around the left shin or hamstring. Keep your back and head flat on the ground while drawing your left shin toward your body, simultaneously pressing your right knee away. Repeat on the other side.

Although you can lift your head while getting into this position, as we are doing in this photo above, once you are in the pose, rest your head on the ground and pull your legs towards your chest (as shown on prior page).

Reclined Twist: *Bharadvajasana*

To perform Reclined Twist, begin by lying on your back on the mat. Bring one knee towards your chest, hugging it gently. Inhale deeply, then exhale as you rotate at the waist, bringing the knee across the body towards the opposite side. Extend your opposite arm out to the side, keeping both shoulders grounded on the mat.

You can gently press down on the knee with your hand to deepen the stretch, but ensure to keep your hips flat on the ground. Repeat on the other side.

When in this twist, anchor the legs while rotating the upper body the opposite direction from the waste. Gently turn your head in the same direction as your upper body for a full spinal rotation.

Happy Baby Pose: *Ananda Balasana*

While on your back, bend your knees toward your chest while keeping your head flat on the mat with the soles of your feet reaching towards the ceiling. Reach forward to grab the inside or outside of your feet, gently spreading your knees apart and bringing them toward your armpits. Ensure your shoulders and head remain firmly on the mat to avoid strain.

If reaching your feet is challenging, consider your holding your shins or thighs for better accessibility.

To truly experience Happy Baby, you have to smile and rock back and forth a little.

Legs Against the Wall: *Virparita Karani*

Lie on your back, ensuring your lower back is pressed into the ground. Extend your legs up the wall, allowing them to rest against it. Relax your arms by your sides with palms facing up. Hold the pose for 3-5 minutes, or as long as you are comfortable.

If you need support for your neck and head, you can use a bolster or small pillow.

Legs Against the Wall not only helps relax the lower back but also assists the lymphatic system by promoting the drainage of lymph fluid from the feet and lower legs.

To get into Legs Against Wall pose, lie sideways to get the legs elevated.

This pose can be particularly beneficial at the end of the day for individuals who spend extended periods standing or sitting at a desk.

Namaste!

The light and life in me sees and acknowledges the light and life in you, and in all humanity.

* * *

Works Cited

Ambreen, G., Siddiq, A. & Hussain, K. "Association of long-term consumption of repeatedly heated mix vegetable oils in different doses and hepatic toxicity through fat accumulation." *Lipids Health Dis* 19, 69 (2020).

Barrett, Julia R. "Chemical Exposures: The Ugly Side of Beauty Products." *Environmental Health Perspectives*, vol. 113, no. 1, 2005, p. A24., doi:10.1289/ehp.113-a24.

Czarneckia, J., Nowakowska-Domagałab, K., & Mokros, Ł. (2024). "Combined cold-water immersion and breathwork may be associated with improved mental health and reduction in the duration of upper respiratory tract infection - a case–control study." *International Journal of Circumpolar Health*, 83, 2330741.

Gearhardt, A., et al. (2023). "Social, clinical, and policy implications of ultra-processed food addiction." *BMJ*, 2023; 383.

Gordon, L.A. (2015). "How lawyers can avoid burnout and debilitating anxiety." *ABA Journal*. July 1, 2015.

Grandner, Michael A. "Sleep Effects on Health and Longevity." *Sleep Medicine Clinics.* 12 (2017): 1-22.

Henderson, K.N.; Killen, L.G.; O'Neal, E.K.; Waldman, H.S. (2021). "The Cardiometabolic Health Benefits of Sauna Exposure in Individuals with High-Stress Occupations. A Mechanistic Review." *International Journal of Environmental Research and Public Health.*

Joicy, M. S., Shetty, G. B., Sujatha, K. J., & Shetty, P. (2021). "Effect of Neutral Immersion Bath with Epsom Salt on Hypertensive Individuals." *Indian Journal of Integrative Medicine*, 1(3), 75-79.

Kawa, M., Orłowski, K., & Kowza-Dzwonkowska, M. (2015)."

The role of myofascial massage in spinal pains in professionally active women." *Balt J Health Phys Act,* 7(4), 85-92.

Lemole, G. M. (2021). *Lymph & Longevity: The Untapped Secret to Health.* Scribner.

Love, H. N. (2017, February 15). "Lawyers are at risk for secondary traumatic stress." *Bar Bulletin,* 56(7).

Lustig, R. H. (2020)." Ultraprocessed Food: Addictive, Toxic, and Ready for Regulation." *Nutrients,* 12(11), 3401.

National Academies of Sciences, Engineering, and Medicine. 2021. *High and Rising Mortality Rates Among Working-Age Adults.* Washington, DC: The National Academies Press. https://doi.org/10.17226/25976.

Pagliai, G., Dinu, M., Madarena, M. P., Bonaccio, M., Iacoviello, L., & Sofi, F. (2021). "Consumption of ultra-processed foods and health status: a systematic review and meta-analysis." *British Journal of Nutrition, 125*(3), 308–318.

Reygaert, Wanda C. "An Update on the Health Benefits of Green Tea." *Oakland University William Beaumont School of Medicine,* Published: 18 January 2017.

Shanahan, C. *Dark Calories: How Vegetable Oils Destroy Our Health and How We Can Get It Back.* Hachette Go, 2024.

Sinha, A. N., Deepak, D., Gusain, V. S., & Authors. (2013). "Assessment of the Effects of Pranayama/Alternate Nostril Breathing on the Parasympathetic Nervous System in Young Adults." *Journal of Clinical and Diagnostic Research,* 7(5), 821-823.

University of North Carolina Chapel Hill. (May 2021). "Ultra-processed foods: A global threat to public health." *UNC Global Food Research Program.*

Van der Kolk, B. A., Stone, L., West, J., Rhodes, A., Emerson, D., Suvak, M., & Spinazzola, J. (2014). "Yoga as an adjunctive treatment for posttraumatic stress disorder: A randomized controlled trial." *Journal of Clinical Psychiatry,* 75(6), e559-e565.

Worley, S. L. (2018). "The Extraordinary Importance of Sleep." *P&T,* 43(12), 758-763.

Yang, C., Du, Y.-k., Wu, J.-b., Wang, J., Luan, P., Yang, Q.-l., & Yuan, L. (2015). "Fascia and Primo Vascular System." *Evidence-Based Complementary and Alternative Medicine,* 2015.

ACKNOWLEDGMENT

Special thank you to Patrick DiDomenico, who is not only a great fitness model, but whose constant stream of insightful ideas encouraged me to write this book.

ABOUT THE AUTHOR

Kimberly Busch

Kimberly Busch blends her experience as a lawyer with her commitment to wellness, guiding professionals toward a balanced, reduced-stress life. As a certified yoga instructor, personal trainer, and advocate for holistic living, she draws on a deep understanding of the physical and mental demands of the legal profession.

Through her writing, speaking engagements, and workshops for professionals, Kimberly empowers others to integrate mindful movement and healthy habits into their daily routines, fostering resilience and well-being that enrich every aspect of their lives.

* * *

www.ingramcontent.com/pod-product-compliance
Lightning Source LLC
Chambersburg PA
CBHW050651270326
41927CB00012B/2972